MUSIC
for
Special
Kids

of related interest

Let's All Listen
Songs for Group Work in Settings that Include Students with Learning Difficulties and Autism
Pat Lloyd
Foreword by Adam Ockelford
ISBN 978 1 84310 583 1

Making Music with the Young Child with Special Needs
A Guide for Parents
2nd Edition
Elaine Streeter
ISBN 978 1 85302 960 8

Fuzzy Buzzy Groups for Children with Developmental and Sensory Processing Difficulties
A Step-by-Step Resource
Fiona Brownlee and Lindsay Munro
Illustrated by Aisling Nolan
ISBN 978 1 84310 966 2

Pied Piper
Musical Activities to Develop Basic Skills
John Bean and Amelia Oldfield
ISBN 978 1 85302 994 3

MUSIC for Special Kids

Musical Activities, Songs, Instruments and Resources

PAMELA OTT

Jessica Kingsley *Publishers*
London and Philadelphia

Unless otherwise stated, the song cards, note representations, photographs and worksheets are by Pamela Ott.

First published in 2011
by Jessica Kingsley Publishers
116 Pentonville Road
London N1 9JB, UK
and
400 Market Street, Suite 400
Philadelphia, PA 19106, USA

www.jkp.com

Library of Congress Cataloging in Publication Data
A CIP catalog record for this book is available from the Library of Congress

British Library Cataloguing in Publication Data
A CIP catalogue record for this book is available from the British Library

ISBN 978 1 84905 858 2

Printed and bound in Great Britain

ACKNOWLEDGEMENTS

This book is dedicated to the many special individuals I have had the opportunity to work with over the years. You and your families have touched me and moved me with your dedication, compassion and unwavering love for each other despite the challenges you face every day. Through my work with you, you have made me aware of what is truly important in our lives.

TABLE OF CONTENTS

HOW TO USE THIS BOOK

The songs and musical activities in this book are presented through the sections Singing, Song Games, Playing Instruments, Creating Your Own Rhythm Bag, Instrument Games, Rhythm Activities, Using Music to Identify Feelings and Emotions, Moving to Music, Learning Musical Concepts and Quiet Time Activities. Each activity includes objectives, materials needed and set up instructions.

Before teaching a new song or activity, I recommend becoming quite familiar with it yourself. The greatest thing about using music with young children and children with special needs is that you do not need to be a professional musician to present it effectively. Children are generally not critical of a person's pitch or tone. They can, however, sense our comfort level with the material being taught. If we are comfortable and having fun with the musical activity or song, then chances are they will too!

One last thing—I recommend presenting new songs or musical activities slowly to young children. They tend to grow to love a favorite song or musical activity in the same manner as a favorite book. When a song becomes a favorite, they'll want to sing and dance to it over and over and over again. This is a wonderful way for children to repeat and practice the skills presented in a song or musical activity. If too much material is presented at once, children may have a hard time learning a song well enough for it to become a favorite. Remember—take it slow and have fun! You will inspire your children to sing, dance, move and learn!

INTRODUCTION

How did you learn your alphabet? Did you sing it? Do you remember singing, moving and enjoying music as a youngster? Do certain songs evoke memories of a time or place in your past?

Because of the properties and attractiveness of music to so many people, music can be an incredibly effective therapeutic and educational medium for young children and individuals with special needs. While this book does not attempt to train you to become a music therapist (music therapists are required to obtain training through an accredited university, fulfill an internship and become Board Certified), it does give many musical activities, instruments and songs that can be used by parents, caregivers and other therapists to augment the learning process—even if you're not a musician!

In my work as a music therapist, I have witnessed the power of music in enticing children to interact even though interaction is difficult for them, to sing or vocalize when they cannot speak, to reach out to play an instrument when it is difficult for them to move their arms or hands and to express themselves through singing, playing and moving in ways they have not been able to before.

I hope you will find these songs, musical activities and instrument ideas helpful in working with the special child in your life.

Chapter **1**

SINGING

Does the sound of children singing bring a smile to your face? Do certain songs evoke feelings of comfort and familiarity? Do you remember songs from many, many years ago?

Singing with your child is not only enjoyable, but very beneficial. Singing together can stimulate growth in many areas of a child's development and in several areas simultaneously. By singing with your child, you may help stimulate language and communication skills, encourage interaction, assist in learning academic concepts, encourage self expression, increase self esteem, help him relax, and help establish routines. So—how do you choose appropriate songs for your children?

First of all, pay attention to the developmental and speech level of your child. The lower the level, the simpler the song should be. Bombarding a child who is not yet speaking with too many words, a song that goes too fast, or has a complicated arrangement will not encourage participation as readily as a song that has fewer words and sounds and is repetitive.

INCREASING SELF ESTEEM THROUGH MUSIC AND MUSICAL ACTIVITIES

Many individuals with special needs struggle with self esteem, most likely from sensing that their performance in many areas is not at the same level of their peers. This is many times internalized, causing a decrease in self esteem.

Playing music, singing songs and participating in music can be amazing self esteem boosters. I always try to create positive experiences through music for my clients. If increasing self esteem is one of your objectives, then fashion the activity for success. This is not the time to say "No, you didn't play that correctly!" Some of my clients have gone on to learn to play an instrument quite proficiently, but all can experience the joy of making music that sounds good whether individually or in a group!

All of the songs, games and activities in this book can enhance a child's self esteem. To create successful musical experiences for your child, I suggest keeping the following things in mind:

1. Have I chosen an activity that will interest my child?

2. Have I modified the activity to the appropriate level to ensure a successful experience?

3. Am I prepared to modify the activity even more if it appears to be too difficult for my child?

4. Will the music made by my child in this activity be pleasing to him?

5. Have I praised my child for attempting the activity?

I am always so pleased with the look on a child's face when they realize "I *can* do this and it sounds good!"

GIVE YOURSELF A HUG

Another way to increase self esteem through music is to find songs that lift the child up. I wrote a song entitled *Give Yourself a Hug*. The words in the chorus are:

> Be good to yourself in every way,
> Tell yourself that you're OK!
> Be happy 'bout yourself and shout hurray!
> And give yourself a hug today!

The lyrics, melody and chords to *Give Yourself a Hug* can be found in the Sheet Music section at the end of the book.

There are motions to the song and it can be a terrific conversation starter about the special qualities found in each individual. Ask the child what makes him happy about himself and be sure to give him suggestions if he has difficulty coming up with positive attributes.

The following chapters outline some of the different types of songs that can be used to encourage growth in objective areas such as language and communication, interaction, and learning new academic concepts. This book does not provide a comprehensive list of children's songs, but will hopefully give you a repertoire with which to begin. Keeping a good variety will keep the child's attention and can also help you retain your sanity!

HELLO SONGS

Starting a class, session or an organized "music time" with a hello song is a terrific way to capture the children's attention, prepare them for the session, provide structure, establish routine and help them transition into a "listening and learning" mode. Once I choose an appropriate hello song for each child or class, I continue to use that same song each time, as it becomes comfortable and familiar to them. Hello songs can also be used at home to get the attention of active and/or noisy little ones. Instead of calling their name, try singing softly and see if suddenly their attention is focused on you.

A very simple hello song that I frequently use is to the tune of *Goodnight Ladies*. This is quite easy and has few words. After singing to my client, I then encourage him to sing it back to me. Many times I will sing with him, omitting the space for my name and encouraging the vocalization of my name. The lyrics, melody and chords for the *Hello Song* can be found in the Sheet Music section at the end of the book. This song is easy enough that I can encourage the child to strum the autoharp or guitar as we sing *Hello*.

HELLO SONG

to the tune of *Goodnight Ladies*

Hello Andrew. Hello Andrew.
Hello Andrew, how are you today?

There are two other hello songs I commonly use depending on who I am working with. The following hello song is a bit wordier and quite appropriate for a classroom setting.

THIS IS THE WAY WE START THE DAY

to the tune of *Here We Go 'Round the Mulberry Bush*

This is the way we start the day,
Start the day, start the day.

This is the way we start the day,
So early in the morning.

First we smile and say hello,
Say hello, say hello.
First we smile and say hello,
So early in the morning.

Then we sit down quietly,
Quietly, quietly.
Then we sit down quietly,
So early in the morning.

We listen very carefully,
Carefully, carefully.
We listen very carefully,
So early in the morning.

The third hello song is a rap that I came up with for one of my pre-teen clients. His favorite type of music is rap and we play the bongo as we "rap" hello to help us stay on the beat.

 THE HELLO RAP

My name is Anthony and I'm here to say,
It's time for music and I like to play!
Today is Wednesday in the afternoon.
I'm feeling_____, how 'bout you?

If the songs above don't quite fit your needs, try writing some words of your own and sing them to a familiar tune.

OMITTING WORDS OR SOUNDS IN A SONG

This category is fairly broad, but each of these songs contain an omission either by the leader, the child or both. Omissions can trigger an automatic vocalization which can be quite helpful when trying to stimulate communication skills.

To encourage vocalizations in my non-verbal or speech-delayed children, I frequently sing one of their favorite songs with them and then strategically omit a word at the end of a sentence or phrase. This frequently results in a spontaneous vocalization from the child, whether it is a word or a sound—to "fill in the blank." For instance, *The Wheels on the Bus* may be sung like this:

THE WHEELS ON THE BUS

The wheels on the bus go round and round,
Round and round, round and _____
The wheels on the _____ go round and round
All through the _____.

If the child responds with a vocalization, you might try it again omitting more, such as:

The wheels on the bus go _____
Round and _____, round and _____
The wheels on the bus go _____
All through _____.

As the child begins to fill in more "blanks," omit a little more until they can complete a phrase or sentence on their own.

Some omission songs encourage filling the blanks with a motion such as a clap. This type of omission song encourages concentration and coordination. An example of this type of omission song is the childhood favorite *Bingo*.

 ## BINGO

In *Bingo*, one letter is omitted during each verse and replaced with a clap until the last verse, when all letters are clapped instead of sung. If a child has difficulty with this concept, try writing all of the letters on a white board. At the end of each verse, ask the child to cross off the next letter and then practice clapping once for every letter that has an X on it.

B̷ X̷ N G O

Yet another type of omission song that requires concentration and coordination is *John Brown's Baby*. This song is sung to the traditional tune of *John Brown's Body* and omits one additional word each verse, substituting the word with a hand motion.

 ## JOHN BROWN'S BABY

John Brown's baby had a cold upon his chest
John Brown's baby had a cold upon his chest
John Brown's baby had a cold upon his chest
And they rubbed it with camphorated oil.

Verse 2: Omit "baby" throughout and do the motion

Verse 3: Omit "baby" and "cold" and do the motions

Verse 4: Omit "baby," "cold" and "chest" and do the motions

Verse 5: Omit "baby," "cold," "chest" and "rubbed" and do the motions

Verse 6: Omit "baby," "cold," "chest," "rubbed" and "camphorated oil" and do the motions.

Motions

- **baby:** rock baby in arms

- **cold:** sneeze

- **chest:** slap chest

- **rubbed:** rub chest

- **camphorated oil:** hold nose and make a face.

REPLACING WORDS WITH SYLLABLES OR SOUNDS IN FAMILIAR SONGS

Many children, even those who are non-verbal or speech-delayed may recognize and find comfort in hearing familiar songs. Unfortunately, many familiar songs (even children's songs) have a lot of words and a tempo that may discourage them from trying to sing. In this case, replacing the words with a syllable or a simple word and slowing the tempo may increase participation.

THE DOO DOO SONG

A little girl I worked with had difficulty with speech due to low tone in her facial muscles. She loved the song *Turkey in the Straw* and would begin to dance every time I played it, but she would not attempt to sing it. I began singing the song slowly using only the sound "doo" and she immediately began to try and sing the sound with the melody. From then on, we sang *The Doo Doo Song* at every session! The lyrics, melody and chords for *Turkey in the Straw* (or *The Doo Doo Song*) can be found in the Sheet Music section at the end of the book.

Other songs that work well with this technique are *Skip to My Lou, Yankee Doodle,* and *Mary Had a Little Lamb.* I have even used it with the melody of *Ode to Joy*! The lyrics, melody and chords for *Ode to Joy* can be found in the Sheet Music section at the end of the book.

Other sounds that can be used with familiar tunes:

- bah, ma, da, la, ta, pa, wah

- moo, foo, goo, too, doo

- hee, me, tee

- oh, doe, toe, so.

Of course, some of these sounds are harder for children to form and make than others. Be sure to check with your child's speech pathologist to get recommendations regarding the best sound to use with your child.

NONSENSE SONGS

Nonsense songs can be an effective way to encourage vocalization in children with or without language delays. Look for songs that have very catchy melodies and simple lyrics—or just syllables. I've found that these songs sometimes encourage vocal participation from several of my clients who have been reluctant to vocalize—maybe due to the simplicity of the lyrics, sounds or syllables.

The following traditional song called *Dum Dum Da Da* is one that many of you old girl or boy scouts may remember! The lyrics, melody and chords can be found in the Sheet Music section at the end of the book.

 DUM DUM DA DA

Dum dum da da, da
Dum dum da da, da
Dum dum da da dee dum.
Dum dum da da, da
Dum dum da da, da
Dum dum da da dee dum.

Begin by singing the lyrics as written and then sing the melody in the following ways:

1. As a cat (meow, meow)

2. As a dog (ruff, ruff)

3. As a mouse (squeak, squeak)

4. As a lion (roar, roar)

Ask the child or children you are working with to suggest more animal sounds!

HEY BOB A NEEDLE

Another popular nonsense song is *Hey Bob a Needle*. The lyrics, melody and chords for this song can be found in the Sheet Music section at the end of the book.

As the child becomes familiar with this song, try increasing the tempo with each subsequent verse. It is also fun to play a simple rhythm instrument to this tune until the clapping section after "Hey Bob." If that proves too difficult for your child, see if he can just sway back and forth or tap his knees.

WADDLEY AH CHA

Waddley Ah Cha is yet another fun nonsense song. The scout version of this song includes some pretty difficult hand motions to do while singing. The lyrics, melody and chords for this song can be found in the Sheet Music section at the end of the book.

If the child is able to do some hand motions as he sings, start with something simple, such as clapping and then work up to as many combinations of hand motions as the child can successfully complete. Here are the advanced hand motions. The motions start on the first beat of the song:

Motions

- Pat knees two times
- Clap hands two times

- Right hand (RH) waves over left hand (LH) two times

- LH waves over RH two times

- RH touches nose, LH reaches over RH to touch right ear once

- LH touches nose, RH reaches over LH to touch left ear once

- Repeat RH touches nose sequence once

- Repeat LH touches nose sequence once.

CALL AND RESPONSE SONGS

Call and response is a form of music in which one person leads a melody or spoken word with a "call" and others respond. This can take the form of a call with a different answer, or an echo song.

When I think of call and response songs, I think of Ella Jenkins and her song *Did You Feed My Cow?* She also has several wonderful echo songs, such as *Toom Bah Ee Leo* and *Pole Pole.*

Call and response songs provide an opportunity to be creative in the response but can be confusing to little learners with limited communication skills. Echo songs, on the other hand, may encourage more participation because the response is just an echo of what was just sung.

Boom Chicka Boom is a fun "spoken" echo song. The words fall easily into a rhythmic speaking pattern.

 BOOM CHICKA BOOM

I said a boom chicka boom (echo)
I said a boom chicka boom (echo)

I said a boom chicka rocka, chicka rocka, chicka boom (echo)
I said a boom chicka boom (echo)
Oh yeah (echo), uh huh (echo), next time (echo)

Then repeat

- a little softer (echo)

- a little louder (echo)

- a little slower (echo)

- a little faster (echo)

- the end! (echo).

The Bear and *Ravioli* are two other popular echo songs. In both songs, the first lines are echoed and the last lines are sung in unison like this:

THE BEAR

The other day (the other day)
I met a bear (I met a bear)
A great big bear (a great big bear)
Away up there (away up there)
Together: The other day I met a bear, a great big bear away up
there.

The lyrics, melody and chords for *The Bear* and *Ravioli* can be found in the Sheet Music section at the end of the book.

SONGS TO TEACH ACADEMIC CONCEPTS

Melody and rhythm can be powerful tools to assist in the retention of academic concepts that are presented. If you work with children, you are most likely aware of the power of music to enhance the recall of material. Just look at the *ABC Song*. How many of you learned your alphabet by singing it? How many of you still sing through the *ABC Song* in your head when you are alphabetizing something?

Music can assist children in learning and retaining many different concepts such as days of the week, months of the year, number concepts, and science or history facts.

Here are several *Days of the Week* and *Month of the Year* songs that have worked well with my children.

 DAYS OF THE WEEK #1

to the tune of *If You're Happy and You Know It*

Every week has seven days, yes it does (clap, clap)
Every week has seven days, yes it does (clap, clap)
Sunday, Monday, Tuesday, Wednesday, Thursday, Friday,
    Saturday
Every week has seven days, yes it does (clap, clap)

And today is Monday, yes it is (clap, clap)
And today is Monday, yes it is (clap, clap)
And today is Monday, yes today is Monday
And today is Monday, yes it is (clap, clap)

And tomorrow is Tuesday, yes it is (clap, clap)
And tomorrow is Tuesday, yes it is (clap, clap)

And tomorrow is Tuesday, yes tomorrow is Tuesday

And tomorrow is Tuesday, yes it is (clap, clap)

DAYS OF THE WEEK #2

to the tune of *Twinkle, Twinkle Little Star*

Sunday, Monday, Tuesday too.

Wednesday, Thursday just for you.

Friday, Saturday, that's the end.

Now let's sing those days again!

Sunday, Monday, Tuesday, Wednesday, Thursday, Friday,
    Saturday!

DAYS OF THE WEEK #3

to the tune of *The Addams Family*

Days of the week (snap, snap)

Days of the week (snap, snap)

Days of the week, days of the week, days of the week (snap,
    snap)

There's Sunday and there's Monday

There's Tuesday and there's Wednesday

There's Thursday and there's Friday

And then there's Saturday

Days of the week (snap, snap)

Days of the week (snap, snap)

Days of the week, days of the week, days of the week (snap,
    snap).

Another concept that can be readily taught through song is the months of the year. I still remember a song I learned in kindergarten—just a few years ago! It was a song that listed the months of the year to a catchy marching tune—and we would march along as we sang. To physically experience the song and its rhythm and melody probably set it even firmer in my little mind. Wow—the power of music! I still find myself humming it on occasion. The lyrics, melody and chords to *Months of the Year* #1 and #3 can be found in the Sheet Music section at the end of the book.

There are two other versions of *Months of the Year* songs that I have used over the years. Both are set to familiar melodies and quite easy to teach and learn.

 ## MONTHS OF THE YEAR #1

January, February, March and April,
May, June and July.
August, September, October too.
November and December are the twelve months of the year.
Nine months of which are our kindergarten year.

 ## MONTHS OF THE YEAR #2

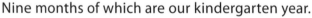
to the tune of *Battle Hymn of the Republic*

January, February, March, April and May,
June, July and August, then September's on the way.
October, then November, then December's at the end.
And we start all over again!

MONTHS OF THE YEAR #3

to the tune of *Michael Finnegan*

January, February, March and April,

May, June, July, August and September,

October, November and December,

These are the months of the year.

THE NAME SONG

Yet another concept that can be taught through music is how to spell a name. The melody and rhythm assist in the retention of the order of the letters. Once learned, the music can quickly be faded out, yet the information should remain. This melody was written to assist both of my children in learning to spell their names and can be adapted to longer or shorter names.

Learning additional concepts through music

This chapter has highlighted the ability to teach concepts by using melody and rhythm to assist in memorization. This can be applied to many other concepts by pairing with a familiar melody, creating your own melody or simply by speaking (or rapping) the information in time.

There are also many entertaining songs readily available for purchase that can assist in memorizing math, science and history facts.

ADAPTING FAMILIAR SONGS

Over the years I have had fun adapting familiar songs to suit my needs. Frequently you can add verses, add a melody to a familiar chant or make other changes that will create a song that will assist in the objective you are seeking to work on.

One of my favorite children's finger play/rhyme songs is *Five Little Monkeys*. Many of the children I work with like this song, but frequently lose interest after the second or third monkey! Plus, I really wanted a song that could provide sequencing opportunities. So—I changed it around—added a familiar melody and verses to make it *Three Little Monkeys*. Now there are hand motions to go with each of the verses and the old standard is new again!

 THREE LITTLE MONKEYS

additional words by Pamela Ott

1. Three little monkeys jumpin' on the bed.
   One fell off and bumped his head!

Momma called the doctor and the doctor said,

"No more monkeys jumpin' on the bed!"

2. Two little monkeys sitting in a tree.

    One fell out and skinned his knee!

    Momma called the doctor, quick as can be,

    And he said "No more monkeys sitting in a tree!"

3. One little monkey swimming in the river.

    Got so cold he began to shiver.

    Momma called the doctor, whose chin began to quiver.

    He said "No more monkeys swimming in the river!"

4. Three sick monkeys, all of them little.

    Lying there in the hospital.

    Lulah and Johnnie and sister Fred, say

    Never again will we swim in the river,

    Or sit in a tree, Or jump on the bed!

    We don't want to bump our head,

    So no more jumpin' on the bed!

Everyone knows the words to Eency Weency Spider.

EENCY WEENCY SPIDER

additional words by Pamela Ott

1. The eency weency spider crawled up the waterspout,

    Down came the rain and washed the spider out.

    Out came the sun and dried up all the rain,

    And the eency weency spider crawled up the spout again.

2. The eency weency spider crawled up the mighty Alps,

    Down came the snow and rolled the spider down.

When she got to the bottom as dizzy as can be,
The eency weency spider decided she would ski.

3. The eency weency spider crawled out to take a hike.
   The wind began to blow the poor spider out of sight.
   She reached into her pack and pulled with all her might,
   And as the wind blew around her, spidey flew her kite.

4. The eency weency spider crawled back up the water spout.
   Down came the rain and washed the spider out.
   She let out a sigh and put her hands upon her lap,
   And said, "Till the weather gets much better, I think I'll take a nap!"

SING AND READ BOOKS

Sing and read books are a terrific way to encourage communication, stimulate language skills, and to practice reading skills with your child. Rhythm and rhyme are a powerful combination in the acquisition of language skills. By pointing to the words as you sing them, children begin to recognize the words by sight and to learn the rhythm of reading (and speaking). I have worked with several non-verbal children who have spontaneously vocalized while listening to me sing a book—especially if I omit an obvious word at the end of a sentence or phrase.

The following is a list of sing and read books that I have used successfully with my clients:

If You're Happy and You Know It—Jane Cabrera (published by Holiday House 2005)

Five Little Ducks—Raffi (Crown Books 1999)

I've Been Working On the Railroad—Ann Owen (Picture Window Books 2006)

The Ants Go Marching—Ann Owen (Picture Window Books 2006)

The Wheels on the Bus—Raffi (Random House 1999)

I'm a Little Teapot—Iza Trapani (Charlesbridge Publishing 1998)

Going On a Train—Pamela Ott (Music Speaks Publishing at www. musicforspecialkids.com)

There are several qualities that I try to identify before purchasing a new sing and read book, and they are as follows:

1. It should have a melody that my children can readily learn.

2. It should be repetitive.

3. The pictures should give clues to the meaning of the text.

4. The font should be big enough that the children can follow along with their fingers.

Many sing and read books are available at local libraries which could allow you to try different titles to see which are most effective and entertaining.

I'm going on a train to see my grandma
Going on a train to see my grandma
Going on a train to see my grandma

SONG CARDS

Using song cards can stimulate interaction and facilitate making choices. On each card, I have up to six pictures that indicate six different songs. Start by helping the child identify the song depicted in each picture by singing the first line as you point to a picture. Once he has connected the song to the picture, you can use the song cards to help a non-verbal child or a child who has difficulty making choices choose a song to sing or play.

Song cards can be easily assembled using clip art found on the computer. Try to find an image that will depict each song. I recommend laminating each sheet for durability.

ABC Song

The Wheels on the Bus

Five Little Monkeys

The Crocodile

Little Bunny Foo Foo

Where is Thumbkin?

Individual song cards

Individual song cards may also be useful when working with children. Create individual song cards by taking a large copy of a song card, then cutting out the individual songs.

Chapter **2**

SONG GAMES

Song games are games based on the use of various components of music such as the melody, rhythm and lyrics. The following games make use of these components to encourage listening and attending skills, sequencing skills and interaction.

Start with easy melodies or well-known songs for maximum interaction and then, if needed, increase the level of difficulty by introducing more difficult melodies or songs that are not as familiar to the child.

WHAT'S THAT SONG? GAME

Objectives: To increase listening skills, attending skills, and interaction.

Materials needed: Individual song cards, a CD or MP3 player with songs represented on the individual song cards. If you feel comfortable, you may just sing or hum the songs instead of playing them on the CD or MP3 player.

Set up: The adult and child should sit on opposite sides of a small table.

Steps

1. Arrange two or more individual song cards on a table in front of the child.

2. Play or sing part of a song and ask the child to identify the song by pointing to the correct card.

3. Ask the child if he would like to sing part of a song for you to see if you can pick the correct song card.

Hint: Make the game easier by using fewer cards and singing more of each song. Make the game more challenging by using more cards and singing less of each song or just humming the song.

 SONG PUZZLES

Choose one of your child's favorite songs. Print the lyrics in large font on a sheet of paper. Cut the song into strips by sentence. Take the song strips and mix them up on a table in front of your child. Encourage him to put the sentences in the correct order. Use singing prompts to assist him.

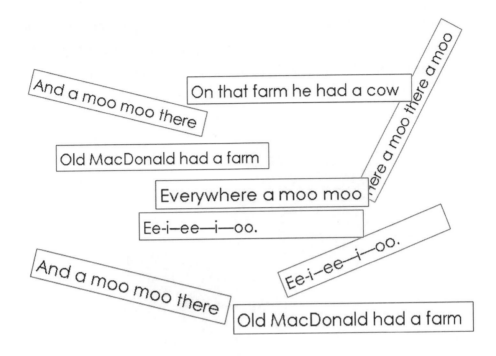

 SINGING AND SEQUENCING

Sequencing can be a difficult concept for little learners. The following game makes use of melody to help the child predict what should come next.

A variety of objects can be used when making a sequencing strip, from fruit to toys to musical instruments. Choose items from the same group to assist in item recognition.

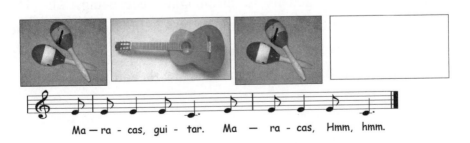

Ma — ra - cas, gui - tar. Ma — ra - cas, Hmm, hmm.

Sing the name of the items using an easy melody—using the same notes for like items (see the melody on p.45). Instead of singing the name of the missing item, hum the note. Make smaller cards of each item and allow the child to choose the picture of the missing instrument and place it in the empty box.

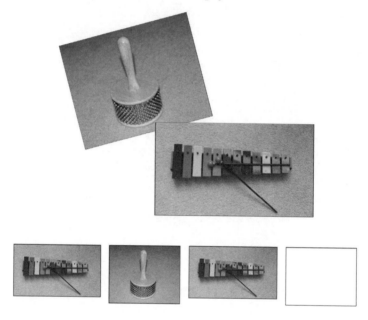

HEAD, SHOULDERS, KNEES AND TOES MIX UP GAME

Head, Shoulders, Knees and Toes is a well known song that can be turned into a fun activity to encouraging sequencing skills. The activity can also be used to encourage the ability to be flexible and take things out of order. On separate cards, print a picture of each body part named in the song and laminate them for durability.

Toes

Nose

Knees

Mouth

Shoulders

Ears

Head

Eyes

Ears

Eyes

Knees

Head

Nose

Mouth

Toes

Shoulders

Objectives: To increase sequencing skills, attending skills, interaction, and flexibility.

Materials needed: Separate cards with a picture of a head, shoulders, knees, toes, eyes, ears, mouth and nose.

Set up: I find this is best played with one adult and one child. The adult should sit with the child at a table or on the floor.

Steps

1. Sing the song *Head, Shoulders, Knees and Toes*.

2. Set out all of the cards in the order they are sung in the song.

3. Sing the song again, this time pointing to each card as you sing the corresponding body part.

4. Mix up the cards and explain to the child that you are going to sing the song in a new order.

5. Point to the cards and sing the song.

6. Ask the child if he would like to mix up the cards and create a new order to sing!

SING AND WHISTLE GAME

Objectives: To increase vocal skills, listening skills, impulse control, attending skills, and interaction.

Materials needed: A large mirror that you can sit in front of with the child, safe whistles for children.

Set up: I find this is best played with one adult and one child. The adults should sit with the child on the floor or on a chair facing a mirror. One whistle should be set in front of the adult and one in front of the child. The adult should ask the child not to touch the whistle yet.

Steps

1. Sing a short vocal exercise (see below) to the child while looking in the mirror and ask him to sing it back to you.

2. Tell the child you are going to sing the vocal exercise one more time together and then you both will get to blow your whistle.

3. Upon completion of the short vocal exercise, allow the child to pick up the whistle and blow. It is usually best to allow a certain amount of time to blow or to identify the number of blows!

Hint: Be sure to find child-safe whistles that cannot be swallowed and whistles that have a softer sound so as not to hurt children's ears.

Ooh,   ooh,   ooh,   ooh,   Ah————————!

Chapter **3**

PLAYING INSTRUMENTS

It seems nearly impossible for a child to walk by a musical instrument without reaching out to touch and explore the sounds it makes. Musical instruments can entice a child to participate and provide a multitude of experiences involving many of the senses.

Developmentally appropriate musical instrument activities can stimulate development in areas such as fine and gross motor skills, eye–hand coordination, interaction, listening skills, and can provide tactile, auditory, and visual stimulation and opportunities for self expression.

Do you need to be a musician to work with children and instruments? Well, if you are going to teach a child how to play an instrument through lessons, then probably yes. But if your goal is simply to provide musical activities for your child that will enhance and stimulate learning experiences, it may be sufficient to simply equip yourself with enough knowledge of the instrument to introduce activities with confidence and enthusiasm and to be able to modify the experience if needed.

Gathering Drum

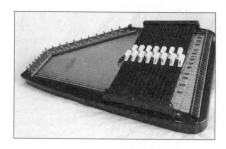

Autoharp

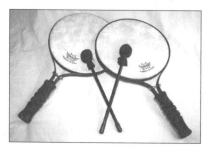

Paddle Drums

Keyboard

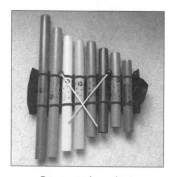

Boomwhackers

Handbells

Q-chord

Glockenspiel

When choosing instruments, be sure to obtain a high enough quality instrument that it produces a pleasant sound. Some instruments bought at discount stores will have little sound or the sound can be very tinny or unpleasant. No one wants to spend much time playing an instrument that doesn't sound good!

The following activities are divided by instrument, include possible objectives, materials needed, set up and activity instructions (steps).

GATHERING DRUM

I like to use the Remo gathering drum (7.5 x 22 inches or 19 x 55 cm). It is big enough for several people to play at the same time and has a very low, rich tone. The drum can be played with hands or with mallets and even—as you will see—with balls!

 ## PLAY—STOP GAME

Objectives: To increase attending skills, interaction, impulse control, and the ability to follow instructions.

Materials needed: Gathering drum, one mallet for each player. Hands can be used instead of mallets.

Set up: This can be played by several children and a leader, or one child and a leader. The child(ren) and leader should sit around the gathering drum with plenty of space to move arms and hands.

Encourage the child to hold the mallet up, as if ready to strike the drum but to wait until you say "play." The leader begins the game by saying "play, play, play, play" then suddenly says "stop!"

Encourage the child to play only when you say "play" and to stop immediately when you say stop. Vary the time that you play before stopping. Once the child understands the concept, ask if he would like to be the leader!

 ## LEARNING OPPOSITES ON THE DRUM

Objectives: To learn the concept of opposites, to increase listening skills, attending skills, interaction, coordination, and motor skills.

Materials needed: Gathering drum, one mallet for each player. Hands can be used instead of mallets.

Set up: This can be played by several children and a leader, or one child and a leader. The children and leader should sit around the gathering drum with plenty of space to move arms and hands.

Steps

1. Play the drum softly and encourage the child to play the same way.

2. Stop playing and tell the child that you are now going to play loud. Model playing loud and ask the child to play the same way.

3. Stop playing and explain that soft is the opposite of loud. Practice the concept by playing soft and then switching to loud.

4. Play softly and ask the child to play the opposite.

5. Play loudly and ask the child to play the opposite.

6. Ask the child if he wants to be the leader.

Repeat this process to work on the opposites fast and slow.

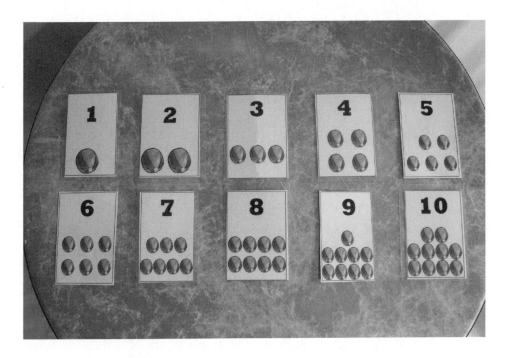

 PRACTICING NUMBER CONCEPTS ON THE DRUM

Objectives: To increase number recognition and numerical concepts, listening skills, attending skills, interaction, coordination, and motor skills.

Materials needed: Number cards for each number 1–10. Number cards can easily be made using clip art on your computer.

Set up: This can be played by several children and a leader, or one child and a leader. The children and leader should sit around the gathering drum with plenty of space to move arms and hands.

Steps

1. Hold up the "1" card. Point to the graphic (in this case a ball) and say "one."

2. Pick up a mallet, hit the drum "1" time and say "one" as you hit it.

3. Repeat the process with the child.

4. If a child is unsure of the concept of seeing a "1" and playing one drum beat, he may need physical assistance. In this case, gently hold the arm holding the mallet, at about the wrist. Guiding his arm, use the mallet to point to the "1" on the card and say "one." Guide his arm to the drum and assist him in playing just one time.

5. Repeat the process with each number card.

6. Once the child has mastered most of the cards, shuffle them and play the game with the numbers out of order.

Hint: You may be able to encourage children who prefer routine and order to play this game "out of order." Mix up the cards and place them face down. Ask the child to choose one or two cards to play. Reward him for successfully completing the request by allowing free play on the drum. Don't force the child to complete the task. If it is too difficult for him at this time, move to another activity and try this one again later.

 GUESS WHICH NUMBER?

Objectives: To increase listening skills, attending skills, and interaction.

Materials needed: Gathering drum, one mallet for the leader, number cards. Hands may be used instead of a mallet.

Set up: This is best played by one leader and one child. The leader and child should sit across the drum from each other.

Steps

1. Lay several number cards face up in front of the child.

2. Ask the child to listen as you play the number of beats on one of the cards in front of him.

3. Ask the child to point to the picture of the number of beats you just played on the drum.

4. Repeat if necessary and encourage the child to count the beats out loud as you play.

Hint: To make this game easier, place only two number cards in front of the child at first and/or play the beats slowly. To make this game more challenging, place more number cards in front of the child and/or play the beats faster.

 COPY CAT

Objectives: To increase attending skills, interaction, impulse control, and the ability to take turns, and to provide an opportunity for self expression.

Materials needed: Gathering drum, one or two mallets for each player. Hands may be used instead of mallets.

Set up: This is best played on the gathering drum by one leader and one child. The leader and child should sit across the drum from each other. To make this a group activity, you may want to provide each person with a smaller drum of their own.

Steps

1. Ask the child to place his hands on his lap and to listen.

2. Play a short pattern such as fast, fast, slow.

3. Ask the child to play back the same pattern.

4. Repeat the pattern if needed.

5. Ask the child if he would like to play a short pattern that you will try to copy!

BALL TOSS ON THE DRUM

Objectives: To increase attending skills, interaction, impulse control, motor skills, and coordination.

Materials needed: Gathering drum, one or two soft balls such as koosh balls.

Set up: This is best played on the gathering drum by one child and one leader. The leader and child should sit across the drum from each other.

Steps

1. Practice tossing the ball to the child by bouncing it once on the drum.

2. Encourage the child to toss it back to you by bouncing it once on the drum.

3. Practice tossing it back and forth with a slow and even rhythm.

4. Start slowly singing a familiar song such as *The Farmer in the Dell*. Begin tossing the ball to the beat of the song. Try to match the bounce of the ball on the drum to the beat of the song.

5. Once the child masters the concept, you can increase the tempo.

Hint: To make this activity more challenging and to increase opportunities for motor coordination and sequencing, add additional steps to this activity. A few examples would be:

Old MacDonald had a farm, EE-I, EE-I, OH
toss - toss - clap   toss-toss-clap

Mary had a lit—tle lamb,   lit—tle lamb, lit—tle lamb
toss - toss - clap - stomp   toss - toss - clap - stomp

 SYLLABLES ON THE DRUM

Objectives: To increase language and reading skills, interaction, impulse control, motor skills, and coordination.

Materials needed: Gathering drum, picture cards of items with varying numbers of syllables (such as ball, apple, elephant, elevator), one mallet for each player. Hands may be used instead of mallets.

Set up: This is best played on the gathering drum by one leader and one child. The leader and child should sit across the drum from each other.

Steps

1. Place one of the picture cards with a low number of syllables next to the drum.

2. Model for the child saying the word syllabically while matching the syllables on the drum.

3. Ask the child to say the word and match the syllables on the drum.

4. Repeat the steps with pictures of words that have more syllables.

Hint: If the child is having difficulty playing and matching the syllables, add the component of melody. Sing the word using a different note for each syllable. So, for the word apple, you could sing "ap" on an "E" and "ple" on a "C."

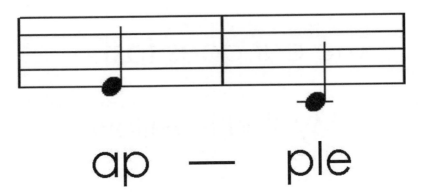

SENTENCES ON THE DRUM

Objectives: To increase language and reading skills, interaction, impulse control, motor skills, and coordination.

Materials needed: Gathering drum, simple sentences printed on strips of paper, one mallet for each player. Hands may be used instead of mallets.

Steps

1. Model reading the sentence slowly and rhythmically.

2. Repeat the sentence again, matching the rhythm of the sentence on the drum simultaneously.

3. Encourage the child to say the sentence and match the beat on the drum.

Hint: To make this activity easier, read the sentence for the child and physically assist them in matching the beat on the drum.

I like music.

The car goes fast.

My shirt is yellow.

BEAN BAG GAME

Objectives: To increase color recognition, impulse control, motor skills, and coordination.

Materials needed: Gathering drum, set of colored bean bags.

Set up: This is best played on the gathering drum by one leader and one to three children. The gathering drum should be placed upside down four or five feet (about 1–1.5 meters) from the children—closer for any children with motor skill challenges.

Steps

1. Scatter the bean bags on the floor.

2. Explain that you are going to sing a song and that the child(ren) should listen and then pick the appropriate bean bag color following the song.

3. Using a simple melody (see p.184) sing "I spy with my eye, a bag that's the color of the grass. Throw it in the drum"

4. Ask one of the children to find the bean bag that is the color of the grass. Then sing "throw it in the drum."

5. Repeat the song for the color of the sky, the color of a pumpkin, the color of an apple, etc.

6. Once the activity is completed, collect the bean bags and ask a child if he would like to be the leader by singing the *I Spy* song to you.

Hint: To make this activity easier, move the drum closer. To make this activity harder, move the drum farther away or use more difficult descriptions of colors in the song!

AUTOHARP

An autoharp is a stringed instrument with attached chord bars which are pressed to play the desired chord. Autoharps come with bars for 15 or 21 chords. I've found that the autoharps with 15 chords provide ample opportunities when working with children.

Autoharps are commonly held against the chest when played by professional musicians. When working with children, I usually place the autoharp on a table or on the floor between myself and a student or place it on my lap or on my student's lap. Many children like to feel the vibrations of the autoharp as it is strummed while on their lap, although children with tactile sensitivities may prefer to play the autoharp when it is not on their lap.

Autoharps are commonly played using picks. Regular guitar picks require good fine motor skills to hold tight enough to strum. If the regular guitar pick is too small for your child to hold, check with your local music store or online for a "monster pick." These picks are about four inches (10 cm) and may provide success for children who struggle to hold the smaller pick.

 ## COUNTING THE STRINGS

Objectives: To increase counting skills, attending skills, interaction, motor skills, and coordination.

Materials needed: Autoharp, guitar pick.

Set up: The autoharp should be placed between the leader and the child. If the child is right handed, the autoharp should be turned so the stringed portion is on their right-hand side. It should be reversed for a child who is left handed.

Steps

1. Take the guitar pick and pluck the string closest to you, counting one.

2. Pluck the next string and count two.

3. Continue plucking and counting until you reach the last string.

4. Start over and encourage the child to count with you as you pluck each string.

5. Ask the child if he would like to hold the pick and pluck each string as you count.

6. Ask the child to pluck each string and count on his own, giving verbal and physical prompts when needed.

 LEARNING THE MUSICAL ALPHABET ON THE AUTOHARP

Objectives: To increase A—G letter recognition, attending skills, interaction, motor skills, and coordination.

Materials needed: Autoharp, guitar pick, 3 x 5 inch (8 x 13 cm) cards with the letters A—G.

Set up: The autoharp should be placed between the leader and the child. The autoharp should be turned so that the letters on the chord bars can be read by the child.

Steps

1. Start with the card with the letter A. Pick up the card, show the child and ask the child to press the chord bar with the A.

2. While the child presses the A chord bar, strum the autoharp.

3. Repeat for the remaining letters.

 ## PLAYING WORDS ON THE AUTOHARP

Objectives: To increase word recognition, attending skills, interaction, motor skills, and coordination.

Materials needed: Autoharp, guitar pick, 3 x 5 inch (8 × 13 cm) cards with any words you can make using the letters of the musical alphabet A—G, such as:

- ACE
- ADD
- AGE
- BAD
- BAG
- BEG
- BEAD
- BED
- CAB
- CAGE
- DAB
- DEAF
- EGG
- FACE

- FAD

- FED

- FEED

- GAB

Set up: The autoharp should be placed between the leader and the child. The autoharp should be turned so that the letters on the chord bars can be read by the child.

Steps

1. Choose one of the cards with a word and show the child.

2. Ask the child to press the chord bar containing the first letter of the word.

3. As the child presses the chord bar for the first letter, strum the autoharp one time.

4. Repeat for the remaining letters of the word.

5. Repeat the word, but this time, simply point to the letter and strum as soon as he matches it. Continue through the letters for the rest of the word.

 PLAYING A SONG ON THE AUTOHARP

Objectives: To increase attending skills, interaction, motor skills, and coordination.

Materials needed: Autoharp, guitar pick, song lead sheet.

Set up: The autoharp should be placed on a table between the leader and the child and turned so that the letters on the chord bars can be read by the child.

Steps

1. Pick an easy two chord song that the child is familiar with, such as *Skip to My Lou*. Put the song lead sheet on the side of the autoharp with the chord bars (see songs below).

2. Start from the beginning of the song. Point to each chord and ask the child to press the chord bar when you point to it.

3. Start from the beginning of the song again and this time, point to the chord with your left hand. When the child presses the chord, strum the autoharp with a pick in your right hand.

4. Repeat step 3, but this time sing the song as you point and strum.

 SKIP TO MY LOU

C
Skip, skip, skip to my Lou
G
Skip, skip, skip to my Lou
C
Skip, skip, skip to my Lou
G   C
Skip to my Lou my darlin'.

TWINKLE, TWINKLE LITTLE STAR

C   F C G C G C
Twinkle, twinkle little star, how I wonder what you are
C   G   C C   G C
Up above the world so high, like a diamond in the sky
C   F C G C G C
Twinkle, twinkle little star, how I wonder what you are.

Hint: To make this activity easier for the child, encourage him to simply strum the strings with a pick as you press the chord bars and sing the song.

PADDLE DRUMS

Paddle drums come in a variety of sizes. The larger the head, the deeper the sound (and the heavier the instrument). I love the deep sound of the 14 inch (35 cm) drum, but find it is sometimes too heavy for my younger clients to hold. I tend to use my two 8 inch (20 cm) drums and two 10 inch (25 cm) drums. The best thing about paddle drums is that they have a handle and can be used in ways that standard drums cannot.

There are many different options for playing paddle drums and this allows you to tailor the experience based on your child's needs.

PLAYING PADDLE DRUMS

Objectives: To increase interaction, impulse control, listening skills, motor skills, and coordination.

Materials needed: Paddle drums, mallets.

Set up: The leader sits on the floor or on a chair facing the child.

Steps for Variation 1 (*One paddle drum—no mallet*)

1. Start by holding one paddle drum horizontally between you and the child.

2. Begin to explore the sound of the drum by asking the child to tap the head of the drum with his fingers.

3. Move the drum side to side and ask him to follow the drum and continue tapping.

4. Move the drum slowly up then down and ask the child to follow the drum and continue tapping.

Steps for Variation 2 (*One paddle drum—one mallet*)

1. Start by holding the drum horizontally between you and the child.

2. Ask the child to tap the drum lightly with the mallet.

3. Follow steps 3 and 4 for *Variation 1* above.

4. Ask the child to hold the mallet in his right hand.

5. Slowly move the paddle drum across your body to the other side.

6. Ask the child to follow and continue tapping the drum.

7. Repeat, asking the child to hold the mallet in his left hand.

Steps for Variation 3 (*One paddle drum—two mallets*)

1. Start by holding the drum horizontally between you and the child.

2. Ask the child to hold one mallet with each hand and lightly tap the drum with both mallets at the same time.

3. Follow steps 3 and 4 for *Variation 1* above.

4. Ask the child to lightly tap the drum alternating between the two mallets.

5. Follow steps 3 and 4 for *Variation 1* above.

6. Hold one mallet and the child holds the other.

7. Tap the drum simultaneously.

8. Tap the drum alternately between yourself and the child.

9. Sing a song and try to match the beat, either by playing at the same time or alternating taps.

Steps for Variation 4 (*Two paddle drums—one mallet*)

1. Start by holding the two drums in a vertical position between you and the child.

2. Ask the child to lightly tap the drums alternating between the two.

3. Slowly move the drums slightly to the left then right. Ask the child to follow and continue tapping the drums alternately.

4. Slowly move the drums up then down. Ask the child to follow and continue tapping the drums alternately.

Steps for Variation 5 (*Two paddle drums—two mallets*)

1. Start by holding the two drums in a vertical position between you and the child.

2. Ask the child to tap a drum with the right mallet and to tap the other drum with the left mallet at the same time.

71

3. Follow steps 3 and 4 in *Variation 4* above.

4. Ask the child to alternate tapping one drum with the left mallet, then the other drum with the right mallet.

5. Slowly move the drums to the left and to the right, asking the child to follow along and continue tapping the drum.

KEYBOARD

Keyboards have become quite popular and are a great alternative to a full size piano for many people. The keyboard can be used to work on many skills and objectives, and many children are very motivated to play it. Unfortunately many parents feel uncomfortable trying to teach any skills on the keyboard because they never learned to play themselves. This chapter is dedicated to introducing some keyboard activities to try with your children—even if you're not a musician!

I would recommend the use of a keyboard that has at least 61 keys—full size keys if possible. I would also guard against the urge to use lighted keyboards. They can be quite over-stimulating for many children.

I created a color chart that I use for the keyboard as seen above. Each key from Middle C to G is assigned its own color and the three notes below middle C have their letter names printed in red. These colors and letters are used in the following activities. You can make a chart like this on your computer and print it on cling paper, or use colored paper and tape to your keyboard. Warning—tape, if left on the keys too long, can damage the surface of the keys. A color strip and color-coded songs can also be purchased and downloaded from *Music for Special Kids* found at www.musicforspecialkids.com

PRACTICING COLOR RECOGNITION ON THE KEYBOARD

Once you have taped the colors to the keys on your keyboard, create cards that coordinate with the keyboard colors. Print colors on regular paper, cut them out in 3 x 5 inch rectangles and laminate each card for durability.

Objectives: To increase color recognition, impulse control, interaction, and motor skills.

Materials needed: Keyboard with color-coded tabs, set of 3 x 5 inch (8 × 13 cm) color-coordinated cards.

Set up: The adult should sit next to the child facing the keyboard.

Steps

1. Depending on the attention span and interest level of your child, choose 1–5 of the colored cards and arrange them on the music stand of your keyboard.

2. Point to the first card and ask the child to play the corresponding colored key on the keyboard.

3. Continue with the rest of the cards on the keyboard.

4. Once mastered, change the order and number of colors until the child is proficient at matching the colors.

5. If they are able, begin to ask the child to point to the colored card on the music stand with the left hand and play the color on the keyboard with the right hand.

6. In preparation of playing full songs on the keyboard, encourage the child to use open fingers and lay them on the keyboard as opposed to using just the index finger with the other fingers curled up under the hand.

 ## PRACTICING LETTER RECOGNITION ON THE KEYBOARD

Another skill that can be developed using the color/letters taped to your keyboard is letter recognition. Print the individual letters of the musical alphabet (A, B, C, D, E, F and G) on cards and laminate them for durability. Make several cards for each letter.

Objectives: To increase letter recognition, impulse control, interaction, and motor skills.

Materials needed: Keyboard with color/letter tabs, set of 3 x 5 inch (8 x 13 cm) letter cards.

Set up: The adult should sit next to the child facing the keyboard.

Steps

1. Place one of the letter cards on the music stand of the keyboard.

2. Point to the card and ask the child to play the corresponding letter on the keyboard.

3. Once all letters are mastered, try combinations of two/three/four letters.

 ## PRACTICING WORD RECOGNITION ON THE KEYBOARD

Once the child has mastered the letter recognition activity, try playing full words!

Words that you can make using the musical alphabet (A, B, C, D, E, F, and G) can be found on pp.66–67. Create word cards using combinations of the individual letter cards.

Objectives: To increase letter and word recognition, impulse control, interaction, and motor skills.

Materials needed: Keyboard with color/letter tabs, set of 3 x 5 inch (8 × 13 cm) letter cards.

Set up: The adult should sit next to the child facing the keyboard.

Steps

1. Place the letters of one of the words or word card on the music stand of the keyboard.

2. Point to each letter and say its name, then say the word.

3. Start again. Point to each letter and ask the child to play the corresponding letter on the keyboard.

4. Once the above steps are mastered, ask the child to play the letters in sequence. Upon completion, say the word.

 KEYBOARD CONCENTRATION

Many keyboards have a setting with sound effects, animal sounds or instrument sounds. If you have a keyboard that has one of these settings, create a picture card that corresponds with each sound using clip art.

Objectives: To increase reasoning skills, impulse control, interaction and motor skills.

Materials needed: Keyboard with color/letter tabs, set of 3 x 5 inch (8 ×13 cm) picture cards that correspond with a sound effect or instrument bank on the keyboard.

Set up: The adult should sit next to the child facing the keyboard.

Steps

1. Briefly explore the sounds that you will be using on the keyboard.

2. Place one of the picture cards on the music stand of the keyboard.

3. Ask the child the name of the picture on the card.

4. Ask the child to press the key with the sound made by the item on the picture card.

5. Once the child becomes comfortable with locating the sound on one card, add two, then three or four and encourage him to find the sounds in the order presented on the cards on the music stand.

6. Start again and let the child choose and set up some cards!

Hints:

1. If the child has difficulty remembering the key for a sound, encourage him to find a clue on the keyboard, such as the lion sound, which is the key with the red square.

2. If the child has difficulty following the order of sounds on the cards, ask him to physically point to each card prior to finding the corresponding key.

BOOMWHACKERS

Boomwhackers are colorful hollow plastic tubes that vary in pitch depending on length. The longer boomwhackers have a lower tone than the shorter ones.

Boomwhackers are lightweight and can be played by striking them together, on the floor, on your knee, or any hard surface. They can also be played with mallets.

Boomwhackers are sold in different sized sets. I have enjoyed working with the "Whack Pack," a set of eight tubes that comes with a tube holder that keeps them arranged in order and allows easy play with a mallet.

Children are drawn to these colorful tubes that have a hollow melodic tone. With careful guidance to remain in control, activities can be created to encourage motor stimulation, leaning to identify a beat, interaction, impulse control, self expression, and much more.

 BOOMWHACKER CHANT

Objectives: To increase directional concepts, impulse control, and motor coordination.

Materials needed: Two boomwhackers for the leader and for each child.

Set up: If there is more than one child, the adult and children should sit in a small circle, otherwise the adult should sit facing the child.

Steps

1. Instruct the child to listen to the words of the chant and to follow along with the instructions.

2. Begin softly tapping the boomwhackers on the floor, one on the left side and one on the right.

3. Begin chanting the following words:

Let's play the boomwhackers on the floor,
One on each side on the floor, on the floor.
Play them fast, play them slow.
Let's play the boomwhackers on the floor, now STOP!

Now play the boomwhackers on the floor

Both on the left side on the floor. (Do a verse with the right side
too.)

Play them fast, play them slow.

Let's play the boomwhackers on the floor, now STOP!

Let's play the boomwhackers on our knees,

Play them now on our knees.

Play them fast, play them slow.

Let's play the boomwhackers on our knees, now STOP!

Let's play the boomwhackers softly on our head.

Softly play on our head.

Play them fast, play them slow.

Let's play the boomwhackers on our head, now STOP!

Continue to add verses depending on the abilities and interest level of your child such as: on your shoes, way up high, way down low, behind your back, etc. Then, ask the child if he would like to lead the boomwhacker chant!

Hint: This is a good activity to use for crossing the midline. Encourage the child to take the boomwhacker held with the right hand, reach over his body and play on the floor on his left side.

BOOMWHACKER COPY CAT

Objectives: To increase auditory sequencing skills, memorization skills, attending skills, impulse control, and motor coordination.

Materials needed: One or two boomwhackers for the leader and for each child. Mallets may also be used.

Set up: If there is more than one child, the adult and children should sit in a small circle, otherwise the adult should sit facing the child.

Steps

1. Perform a motion or a sequence of motions with the boomwhacker such as tapping two boomwhackers together three times.

2. The child repeats the motion.

3. Ask the child if he would like to be the leader.

Additional motions and sequences

1. Tap a boomwhacker held with the left hand two times on the left side, then a boomwhacker held with the right hand two times on the right side.

2. Tap one boomwhacker on the floor one time, on your knee one time and on your elbow one time.

3. Hold the boomwhackers over your head, tap them together three times, then bring them down low and tap them together three times.

4. Secure the boomwhackers in the cloth holder. Take one mallet and play a sequence, such as tapping the red tube one time, then tapping the yellow tube one time.

Hint: To make this activity easier, use only one boomwhacker and only one or two motions. To make this activity more challenging, use two boomwhackers and longer sequences of motions.

SYLLABLE BEATS ON THE BOOMWHACKERS

Objectives: To increase language skills, impulse control, and motor coordination.

Materials needed: One or two boomwhackers for the leader and for each child. 3 x 5 inch (8 x 13 cm) picture cards of words with varying syllables, such as elephant, apple, drum, jumping, kangaroo, saxophone, guitar, and so forth.

Set up: If there is more than one child, the adult and children should sit in a small circle, otherwise the adult should sit facing the child.

Steps

1. Allow the child to pick one of the cards and place it on the floor between you.

2. Point to the picture and pronounce the word syllabically.

3. Ask the child to play the word with you on the boomwhackers, matching each syllable with a tap of the boomwhacker.

PLAYING A SONG ON THE BOOMWHACKERS

Objectives: To increase eye–hand coordination, fine motor skills, attending skills, impulse control, and self expression.

Materials needed: A set of boomwhackers in a boomwhacker holder, one mallet each for the leader and child.

Set up: The open set of boomwhackers should be laid on a table in front of the child.

Steps

1. Create, purchase or borrow a simple song notated in colors and letters that coordinates with the boomwhackers. (*Old MacDonald* below has the codes for each color written above each word. Printing the words on the computer and colorizing each word is an easier method for the beginning player.)

2. Point to the first note (color) and then tap that color tube.

3. Model this way for the first line of the song.

4. Point to the first note (color) and ask the child to tap that color tube.

5. Continue through the song, pointing to the colors and encouraging the child to tap the corresponding tube.

6. If the child masters the steps above, begin again and try to sing (without pointing to the color) while the child taps each tube. Sing as slowly as necessary to make it a successful activity for the child.

 OLD MACDONALD ON THE BOOMWHACKERS

```
G  G   G R   O   O R    P    P  DG  DG G
Old  MacDonald had a farm, Ee—I—Ee—I—Oo
```

```
G  G  G    R O   O R   P    P  DG  DG G
On that farm he had a cow, Ee—I—Ee—I—Oo
```

```
R   R G   G    G    R   R G    G    G
With a moo moo here, and a moo moo there
```

```
G   G G   G    G G    G  G G    G G   G
```

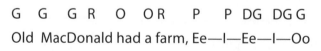

Here a moo, there a moo, everywhere a moo moo.

G   G   G R   O   O R   P   P DG DG G

Old MacDonald had a farm, Ee—I—Ee—I—Oo

Color codes:

R = red	Light Green = G
O = orange	Dark Green = DG
Y = yellow	P = purple

ARRANGING BOOMWHACKERS BY LENGTH

Objectives: To increase sequencing skills and fine motor skills.

Materials needed: A set of eight boomwhackers in varying lengths, the boomwhacker holder.

Set up: The boomwhackers should be laid in a random order in front of the child.

Steps

1. Ask the child to find the shortest boomwhacker and insert it into the first hole on the boomwhacker holder.

2. Ask the child to find the next longest boomwhacker and continue until all boomwhackers are in order in the holder from the shortest to longest.

MAKING LETTERS WITH THE BOOMWHACKERS

Objectives: To increase cognitive skills and motor skills.

Materials needed: A set of eight boomwhackers in varying lengths.

Set up: The boomwhackers should be laid in a random order in front of the child.

Steps

1. Pick up two boomwhackers and make the shape of a V.

2. Ask the child to pick up two boomwhackers and make a V.

3. Repeat, making the shapes of an A, E, F, H, I, K, L, M, N, T, W, X and Y.

Hint: You can do this same activity with rhythm sticks if you have at least four of them.

HANDBELLS

There are some wonderful, affordable handbell sets for children available at many music stores and online. I use the Kidsplay Diatonic 8 note set with the case. It is fairly durable, colorful and the bells have a pleasant tone. Each bell is labeled (on the top of the handle) with its note name and the number in the scale.

Handbells can be a difficult instrument for children with noise sensitivities to tolerate. If you notice your child trying to cover his ears when a bell is played, don't force him to play. Instead, you might set a bell or two in front of him in case he would like to explore at his own pace.

BELL COLOR MATCHING GAME

(Note: You will need to create the color-coded cards to go with the colors of *your* handbell set.)

Objectives: To increase color matching skills, attending skills, and impulse control.

Materials needed: One set of eight handbells, 3 x 5 inch (8 x 13 cm) corresponding color-coded cards.

Set up: I have found this activity to work best with one child and one leader. The leader should sit across from the child with ample room in between to place the bells and the cards.

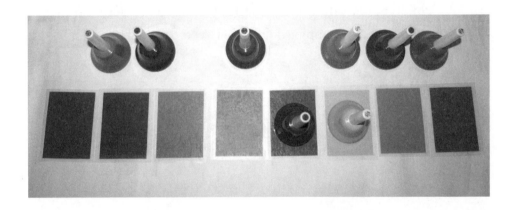

Steps

1. Place the eight color-coded cards in a line in front of the child.

2. Place the eight bells in random order behind the color-coded cards.

3. Point to the first card and ask the child to find the bell that matches that color.

4. When the child locates the bell, ask them to ring it one time then place it on the correct color-coded card.

5. Repeat for the rest of the colors.

 RING THE COLOR GAME

Objectives: To increase color matching skills, attending skills, interaction, and impulse control.

Materials needed: One set of eight handbells, 3 x 5 inch (8 x 13 cm) corresponding color-coded cards.

Set up: This is a good activity for one child and one leader or two children and one leader. The leader should sit across from the child(ren) with ample room in between for the bells.

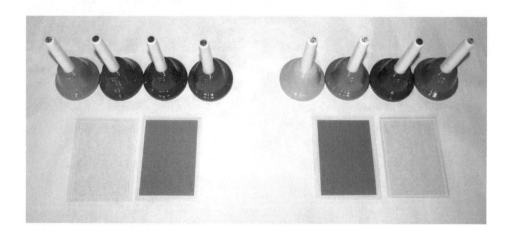

Steps

If playing with one child:

1. Put all the bells in front of the child.

2. Put the color-coded cards face down in two piles in front of you.

3. Turn over the first card and ask the child to find the bell of the same color.

4. Once the bell is found, ask the child to hold the bell, count to three with you—then ring the bell!

5. Repeat for the remaining bells.

If playing with two children:

1. Divide the bells equally in front of both children.

2. Divide the color-coded cards in two piles corresponding with the bell colors in front of each child.

3. Turn both piles of cards over.

4. Take one card from each pile, turn them over and show both children their color-coded card at the same time.

5. Ask both children to find the bell that matches the color on their card.

6. When both children have found their bell, ask the child to hold their bell quietly, count to three with you—then ring the bell!

 ## PLAYING A SONG ON THE HANDBELLS

Playing the melody of a song on the handbells can be a little challenging due to frequent bell changes, although simple melodies certainly can be accomplished by many children. There are also many arrangements available for several players at one time which will decrease the changes each child needs to make. When I use handbells with many of my special needs children I prefer to use the handbell as an accompanying instrument as this simplifies the process and reduces the frequency of bell changes.

Learning to play or accompany a song independently on an instrument can be a terrific self esteem builder for many children and can be a great way to promote interaction though making music together. Learning to accompany a simple song on the handbells can easily be done using color-coded song sheets.

Below are two song sheets that may be used to teach a child to accompany the song *Shoo Fly*. The first one encourages ringing one bell at a time and the second one encourages ringing two bells at once. These sheets are most effective if printed in color. You may wish to re-create these sheets on your computer using just the words and a colored box over the appropriate word of the song indicating which bell to ring.

Shoo Fly (with one accompanying handbell)   traditional

Shoo Fly (with one accompanying handbell)

traditional

Shoo fly, don't bo — ther me. Shoo fly, don't bo — ther me.

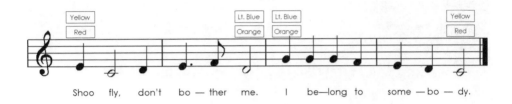

Shoo fly, don't bo — ther me. I be—long to some —bo — dy.

 PUTTING THE BELLS AWAY IN ORDER

The bells are arranged in the case in an up and down order as shown on p.90.

Objectives: To increase sequencing skills, fine motor skills, attending skills, and impulse control.

Materials needed: One set of eight handbells, the carrying case.

Set up: The open case of handbells should be laid on a table in front of the child.

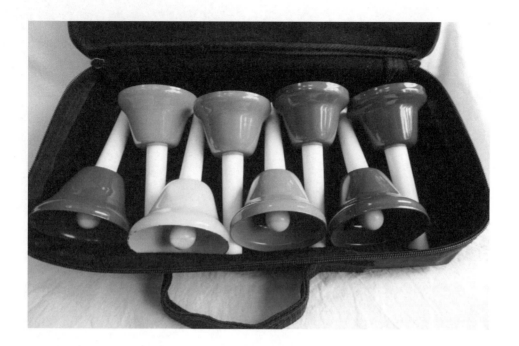

Steps

1. Point to the first bell, saying "down."

2. Point to the second bell, saying "up."

3. Continue through the rest of the bells saying "down, up" in a steady rhythm.

4. Take the bells out of the case and place them in front of the child.

5. Ask the child to put them back in the case in the "down, up" order (don't worry about the alphabetical or numeric order yet).

6. Once the child has mastered the down and up concept, encourage the child to put the bells in the case in the order of the numbers found on the top of the handle.

Q-CHORD

The Q-chord is a portable digital instrument shaped somewhat like a guitar. It can easily be played by pressing a chord button and strumming a finger over the strum plate. There are 36 chords available including major, minor and 7th chords. Ten strumplate voices are available, including guitar, piano, and flute voices. In addition, it contains a rhythm bank with ten different rhythms to play along with and additional cartridges can be purchased to increase the number of available rhythms. There is a volume control and a tempo setting for the rhythms.

The Q-chord uses batteries (which increases its portability) or an AC power adapter. It is fairly light and can be placed in a child's lap for easy playing.

The Q-chord will allow your child to quickly play very professional sounding songs as well as offer a multitude of opportunities to work on academic and motor skills. The sounds are quite pleasant and it seems to be quite motivating to press the buttons. In fact, the hardest thing about using the Q-chord with my children is that it requires some impulse control and it is difficult for some children to concentrate and not push every button. This is a good instrument to award free play time on after completion of a structured activity!

 ## PLAYING A SONG ON THE Q-CHORD

To maximize involvement and interaction, I frequently use the following steps when introducing the Q-chord.

Objectives: To increase fine motor skills, motor coordination, attending skills, impulse control, and interaction.

Materials needed: A Q-chord.

Set up: The Q-chord should be laid on the child's lap, or on the table or floor between the leader and the child. The chord letters should be facing the child.

Steps

1. Pick an easy song that the child is familiar with such as *Mary Had a Little Lamb.* Encourage the child to continually strum his finger over the strum plate as you press the chord buttons and sing.

2. Once the child has become comfortable with strumming, encourage the child to press the chord button while you strum. You may need to point to the chords as you sing the song.

3. If the child is able, begin the song again and encourage the child to press the chords and strum at the same time as you sing the song.

 COMPOSING A SONG ON THE Q-CHORD

The Q-chord is an excellent instrument to use to encourage the child to make up a song of their own.

1. Begin by encouraging the child to choose a topic for the song.

2. Assist them in writing some very easy lyrics pertaining to the topic.

3. Ask the child to pick a rhythm setting.

4. Ask the child to pick three chords to use in the song. Suggested chord families to begin with:

- C, F, G
- G, C, D
- D, G, A
- A, D, E

5. Write chords above the lyrics and then ask the child to play and sing!

Hint: To make this activity easier, encourage the child to just pick a topic and then ask them to play and sing about it.

PRACTICING LETTER RECOGNITION ON THE Q-CHORD

For this activity, use musical alphabet cards (see *Practicing Letter Recognition on the Keyboard* earlier in this chapter for instructions on how to make them p.74).

Objectives: To increase letter recognition, impulse control, interaction, and motor skills.

Materials needed: Q-chord, set of 3 x 5 inch (8 ×13 cm) musical alphabet cards.

Set up: The Q-chord should be placed on the child's lap with the letters of the chords facing the child.

Steps

1. Hold up one of the musical alphabet cards.

2. Point to the card and ask the child to find and press the corresponding letter on the Q-chord and strum the strum plate.

3. Once all letters are mastered, try combinations of two/three/four letters.

 ## PRACTICING WORD RECOGNITION ON THE Q-CHORD

Once the child has mastered the letter recognition activity above, try playing full words!

There is a list of some of the words you can make using the musical alphabet which is A, B, C, D, E, F, and G on p.66–67. Create word cards using those words, or use combinations of the individual letter cards.

Objectives: To increase letter and word recognition, impulse control, interaction, and motor skills.

Materials needed: Q-chord, set of 3 x 5 inch (8 x 13 cm) word cards.

Set up: The Q-chord should be placed on the child's lap with the letters of the chords facing the child.

Steps

1. Place the letters of one of the words next to the Q-chord.

2. Point to each letter and say its name then say the word.

3. Start again. Point to each letter and ask the child to play the corresponding letter on the Q-chord, strumming once after pressing each chord letter.

4. Once the above steps are mastered, ask the child to play the letters in sequence. Upon completion, say the word.

XYLOPHONE OR GLOCKENSPIEL

A xylophone is an instrument in the percussion family comprised of bars of varying lengths which emit different tones when struck with a mallet. Xylophone bars are commonly made of wood while the glockenspiel bars are metal. Glockenspiels usually are smaller than xylophones and have a higher pitch.

Because glockenspiel bars are made of metal, the sound can be sharper and may cause discomfort for some children with auditory sensitivities; however, they tend to be more portable and affordable.

Basic Beat offers a glockenspiel with 12 brightly colored bars. It comes in a set that includes a hard-shell case with magnetic staff board, a set of small magnets, and two sets of mallets. The magnets are small and do present a choking hazard, so this is not recommended for small children—carefully monitor all children when using them. This set is affordable and presents many opportunities to work on academic, fine motor, impulse control, and attending skills.

The following activities are explained using the above mentioned glockenspiel set. Some activities may be modified to accommodate other glockenspiels or xylophones.

 ## MATCHING COLORS ON THE GLOCKENSPIEL

Create cards that coordinate with the bar colors on the glockenspiel. Print colors on regular paper, cut them out in rectangles and laminate each card for durability.

Objectives: To increase color recognition, impulse control, interaction, and motor skills.

Materials needed: Twelve note colored bar glockenspiel, two glockenspiel mallets, set of 3 x 5 inch (8 × 13 cm) color-coordinated cards.

Set up: The glockenspiel should be placed on a table in front of the child.

Steps

1. Depending on the attention span and interest level of your child, choose up to five of the colored cards and place them on the table next to the glockenspiel.

2. Point to the first card and ask the child to play the corresponding colored bar on the glockenspiel.

3. Continue with the rest of the colored cards on the table.

4. Once mastered, change the order and number of colors until the child is proficient at matching each color.

5. If they are able, begin to ask the child to point to the colored card on the table with the left hand and strike the color bar on the glockenspiel with the mallet in the right hand. (Reverse for left-handed children.)

 PRACTICING LETTER RECOGNITION ON THE GLOCKENSPIEL

Print the individual letters of the musical alphabet (A, B, C, D, E, F and G) on cards and laminate them for durability. Make several cards for each letter.

Objectives: To increase letter recognition, impulse control, interaction, and motor skills.

Materials needed: Twelve note colored bar glockenspiel, two glockenspiel mallets or magnets, set of 3 x 5 inch (8 × 13 cm) letter cards.

Set up: The glockenspiel should be placed on a table in front of the child.

Steps

1. Place one of the letter cards on the table beside the glockenspiel.

2. Point to the card and ask the child to play the corresponding letter on the glockenspiel. If using the Basic Beat glockenspiel set, magnets may be placed on the requested letters in place of playing them with the mallet.

3. Once all letters are mastered, try combinations of two/three/four letters.

PRACTICING WORD RECOGNITION ON THE GLOCKENSPIEL

See the instructions for *Practicing Word Recognition on the Q-chord* in the previous section. Using these instructions, substitute the glockenspiel for the Q-chord. If using the Basic Beat glockenspiel set, magnets may be placed on the requested letters in place of playing them with the mallet.

COUNTING THE BARS

Objectives: To increase counting skills, impulse control, interaction, and motor skills.

Materials needed: Twelve note colored bar glockenspiel, one glockenspiel mallet.

Set up: The glockenspiel should be placed on a table in front of the child.

Steps

1. Starting on the lowest bar of the glockenspiel, hit the bar with the mallet saying "one."

2. Moving up the glockenspiel, continue hitting the bars in succession while counting.

Chapter 4

CREATING YOUR OWN RHYTHM BAG

Whenever I work with children, whether in home or in my office, I bring along my "rhythm bag." This is actually my "rhythm instrument bag," but over the years it's been shortened to rhythm bag. Apparently it's just a little easier for my clients (and me!) to say. Plus, the name fits. As I walk down the hall holding my rhythm bag it jingles and jangles, dings and tweets from the combobulation of instruments knocking up against each other. The zipper no longer works and the bag hangs open when I set it on the floor, revealing some very used and loved instruments and enticing my little ones to work hard so they can pick something to play out of Ms. Pamela's rhythm bag.

I've been asked by parents, teachers and therapists what instruments they should get to put together their own rhythm bag. The answer of course is that it depends on the child(ren) you are working with and what objectives you hope to accomplish. That said, here are some recommendations.

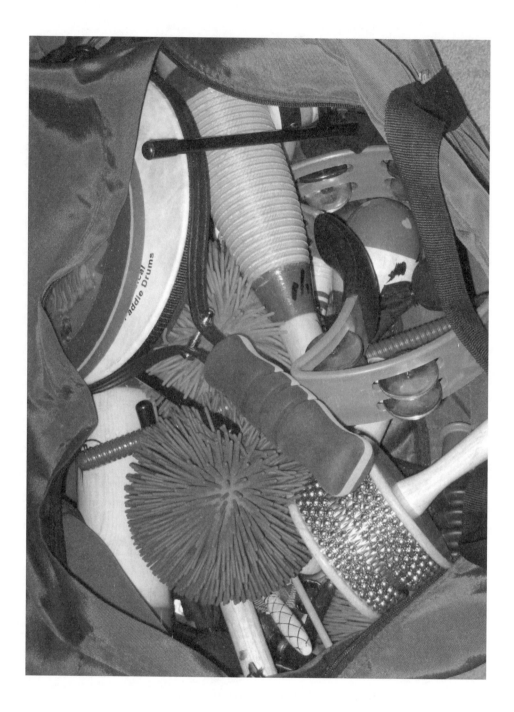

Cabasa

Egg Shakers

Ocean Drum

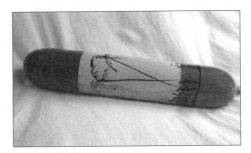

Rainstick

Finger Castanets

CABASA

The cabasa is a percussion instrument that makes a metallic, rattling type of sound when shaken or twisted. It provides a cool, slightly bumpy sensation that can usually be well tolerated by children with tactile sensitivities.

 ## CABASA ACTIVITY

1. When exploring the cabasa with your child, allow him first to hold it and control the amount of sound that it makes.

2. Once he feels comfortable with that, encourage him to cup his hands around the metal balls while you turn the handle.

3. If he is comfortable, see if you can gently run the cabasa up the inside of his arm to his elbow.

4. Then, ask if he would like to run the cabasa up your arm!

EGG SHAKERS

Egg shakers can be constructed of wood or plastic. I selected the Basic Beat egg shakers because of the vibrant colors, they are easy and comfortable to hold and they sound really good. The sound is easily tolerated by most of my children with sound sensitivities and they provide a nice tactile sensation, yet are light and easy to hold.

Egg shakers can be held in the palm of your hand or between fingertips and thumbs. I keep four egg shakers in my rhythm bag so I can give the child I am working with two of them and I can play the other two.

Egg shakers are relatively inexpensive and small. They work well in group activities, so if you work with a group you could easily keep eight or more in your bag.

EGG SHAKER ACTIVITY

1. Play copy cat with the shakers. Start with an easy pattern such as "shake, shake, knee, /tap the shakers on your knee/" and see if the child can copy your motions.

2. Once that motion is mastered, move up to motions with more steps such as "shake, shake, knee, knee, toes, toes" or more difficult steps such as "shake, knee, high, low."

OCEAN DRUM

There are many different styles and sizes of ocean drums. The larger ocean drums are heavier, but have a bigger sound which provides more auditory and tactile stimulation. The smaller ocean drums are lighter and are easier for some small children to hold and maneuver.

If you gently rock the ocean drum from side to side, the beads provide a mesmerizing and pleasant sound somewhat like ocean waves. The ocean drum can also be tapped with a finger or hand or tapped on a knee. This instrument provides a pleasant auditory and tactile experience.

The only drawback with the ocean drum is that it can be over-stimulating for some children who may have difficulty attending or interacting while playing the instrument. If you find that to be the case with your child, you may elect to use the ocean drum as a reinforcement or reward for the completion of a separate activity.

RAINSTICK

Rainsticks come in many different lengths, shapes and sizes. Many rainsticks are made from cacti. Nails, cactus spines or pegs are affixed to the inside of the rainstick, then pebbles, beans, seeds or other small items are added. When the rainstick is gently tilted, the pebbles or other small items fall past the pegs and create a rushing sound like rain.

Rainsticks are terrific instruments to use when working on objectives such as motor coordination and motor control. The smaller the rainstick, the easier it is to control and to create a consistent rain sound. Longer rainsticks are heavier and harder to control, but can provide a longer rain sound with good control.

FINGER CASTANETS

Castanets are percussion instruments that are commonly made of hardwood. Some castanets are made of colorful plastic and work quite well for children.

Finger castanets can be an excellent instrument to use to stimulate fine motor skills.

 FINGER CASTANET ACTIVITY

1. Allow the child to pick a favorite castanet.

2. Hold your castanet between your thumb and pointer finger and click the castanet together. Ask the child to copy you.

3. Repeat with the thumb and middle finger, thumb and ring finger and thumb and pinky.

4. Hold your castanet in the palm of your hand and use all the fingers at the same time to click the castanet. Try using separate fingers too.

5. Hold your castanet in the palm of your hand and use all the fingers of the opposite hand to click the castanet. Try using separate fingers too.

6. Take turns. Ask the child to pick a way to play the castanet and copy him!

For children who have difficulty holding and playing a finger castanet, try a castanet with a handle.

Cowbell

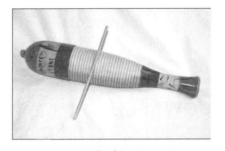

Guiro

Claves

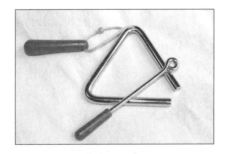

Triangle

Rhythm Sticks

Wrist Bells

Maracas

Tambourine

COWBELL

The cowbell instrument is made of metal and is missing the clapper that was present in the actual bells used for herding cows.

The cowbell can be struck with a stick providing a sharp tone. The tone can be dampened with the hand. For a softer tone, try using a rubber mallet.

GUIRO

The guiro is an instrument made from a hollowed gourd, wood or plastic. The guiro has a grooved surface which when scraped with a stick produces a rasping sound.

The guiro provides an interesting tactile sensation in both the hand holding it and the hand holding the stick as it scrapes across the grooved surface. The guiro also provides a different auditory sensation than most of the other instruments outlined.

CLAVES

Claves are percussion instruments fashioned out of short pieces of rounded wood. When hit together they create a clicking noise. They are easy to grasp and provide a pleasant percussive sound.

TRIANGLE

The triangle is a popular percussion instrument that can be a good addition to your rhythm bag. The triangle provides the opportunity to work on several objectives such as developing fine motor skills, increasing motor coordination, and decreasing auditory sensitivities.

To play the triangle, hold a bar or loop that is attached to the top of the triangle with one hand and strike the triangle with the beater held in the other hand. The triangle can also be suspended from a music stand.

The sound of a triangle can be described as sharp or tinny and can cause over-stimulation in children with auditory sensitivities. If your child appears over-stimulated by the triangle, don't force him to play. Instead, show him how to make a very soft sound and see if he would like to hold and explore it.

RHYTHM STICKS

These simple wooden sticks with ribs provide both an auditory and tactile sensory experience. They can be played by rubbing them together or gently hitting them together.

WRIST BELLS

Wrist bells are bells affixed to a fabric or plastic strap that can be worn on the wrist. This type of bell is extremely useful for children who have motor challenges. You can also find bells affixed to a strap with Velcro that can be worn around the ankle.

MARACAS

This popular percussion instrument is fashioned from a gourd, or more recently wood or plastic, and filled with dried beans or seeds. Maracas are frequently played in pairs, either one in each hand or two in one hand. Maracas are usually shaken, but can also be gently tapped on a leg or the palm of a hand.

TAMBOURINE

This popular percussion instrument consists of a frame with metal jingles. Some tambourines have drum heads and some have open heads. Tambourines come in various shapes and sizes. The tambourine you choose should be light and easy for your child to hold. Tambourines can be shaken or tapped and provide a pleasant, sharp sound.

PERCUSSION INSTRUMENT ACTIVITIES

Percussion instruments provide tremendous auditory and tactile sensation and can be used in a rhythm band or in the following activities:

1. Encourage the children to play the instrument to the beat of a song. Try a fast paced song—then a slower one. If this concept is difficult for them, play with them on the same instrument and count or identify the beat by making a vocal sound on the beat as you play.

2. Ask the child if he can play LOUD—then soft.

3. Ask the child to play high—then low.

4. Play your instrument fast—then ask the child to play the opposite. Repeat for loud—soft and high—low.

5. To encourage interaction on the rhythm sticks, hold your sticks in front of the child and ask him to play his sticks on yours. Move your sticks higher or lower and encourage him to follow.

Chapter **5**

INSTRUMENT GAMES

HIDE AND SEEK WITH INSTRUMENTS

Objectives: To increase attending skills and interaction.

Materials needed: Rhythm instruments, 3 x 5 inch (8 x 13 cm) rhythm instrument picture cards.

Set up: This can be played by one child and one leader; however, playing with several children and one leader can offer opportunities for learning to take turns.

Steps

1. Take a picture of each instrument or find a clip art picture of the instrument on the internet. Create cards, each with a picture of one of the instruments.

2. Lay the pictures of the instruments in a row on the floor or on a table.

3. Encourage the child to close his eyes while you hide the instruments in the room.

4. Once hidden, ask the child to find each of the instruments and place it on its picture.

Hint: To make this game easier, use fewer instruments. To make it more challenging, use more instruments and harder hiding places!

NAME THAT INSTRUMENT

Objectives: To increase attending skills, interaction, auditory awareness, and instrument identification.

Materials needed: Rhythm instruments, 3 x 5 inch (8 x 13 cm) rhythm instrument picture cards.

Set up: This can be played by one child and one leader; however, playing with several children and one leader can offer opportunities for learning to take turns.

Steps

1. Place the pictures of the instruments in a row on the floor or on a table.

2. Ask the child to sit facing the cards.

3. Sit behind the child with access to each of the instruments.

4. Pick one of the instruments and play it.

5. Ask the child to identify the instrument by pointing to its picture.

6. Continue for the rest of the instruments.

Hint: To make this game more challenging, play the instrument for a shorter time before asking the child to identify it, or ask the child to identify the instrument by name.

 TWISTER INSTRUMENTS

Objectives: To increase motor coordination, attending skills, interaction, impulse control, and the ability to take turns.

Materials needed: A Twister game, rhythm instruments, 3 x 5 inch (8 x 13 cm) rhythm instrument picture cards.

Set up: This game can easily be played by several children and one leader.

Steps

1. Spread a Twister game mat on the floor.

2. Set the instrument cards upside down next to the Twister spinner.

3. Ask the child to spin the spinner.

4. When it stops, ask the child to identify the color it landed on.

5. Pick the instrument card on the top of the pile and turn it over.

6. Ask the child to pick up the instrument pictured on the card.

7. Standing on the edge of the Twister mat, ask the child to step one foot at a time down the colored dots identified on

113

the spinner while playing the instrument identified on the card.

8. The next child then takes a turn while the others watch.

Hint: To make this activity more challenging, change the way the player moves down the dots, for example hop, walk backwards, turn around and around.

Chapter **6**

RHYTHM ACTIVITIES

We are exposed to rhythm even before we are born through the gentle rhythmical pulsations of our mother's heartbeat.

Rhythm is a great organizer and is not only found in music, but is present in everyday speech and movement. For children with challenges in these areas, rhythm may assist in the coordination of these systems.

When I began working with special needs children, I introduced them to rhythm primarily through auditory exercises. I soon found that many of the children I worked with not only could benefit from learning rhythm through note values, many excelled at it! My goal was to use music to work on non-musical objectives, and in the process, many of them began to learn note names and notated rhythm!

I was familiar with the Kodaly method of notation (ta, ta, ti, ti) and although this method works quite well with many children, I found I needed to make some modifications to fit the needs of my students. For instance, the Kodaly whole note is counted "ta-a-a-a."

I modified the whole note to "ta—2, 3, 4," as this seemed to help children to remember where they were in the beat sequence.

After learning the patterns on the following pages, we began to combine the rhythmic pattern with movement, thereby solidifying it even more in the memory.

INDIVIDUAL NOTE CARDS

Before moving to the rhythm worksheets, make individual note cards as shown on p.117. Lamintae them for durability and make several copies of each so that you have more cards to work with.

 ## LEARNING THE NOTE VALUES

Objectives: To increase the ability to decode symbols, visual tracking, eye–hand coordination, and interaction skills.

Materials needed: Individual laminated note cards.

Set up: When first learning the note values, this activity is recommended for one student and one leader. The student and leader sit across and facing each other either on the floor or at a table.

Steps

1. Place the card with a picture of a quarter note in front of the child.

2. Point to the note and say "ta."

3. Ask the child to point to the note and say "ta."

4. Clap one time and say "ta."

5. Ask the child to clap one time and say "ta."

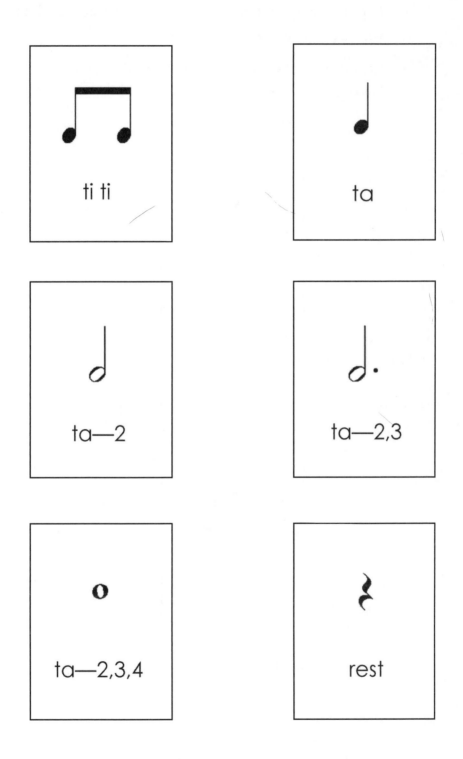

6. Explain that every time they see the quarter note card, they will clap one time while saying "ta."

7. Repeat the above steps for the remaining note cards (see below).

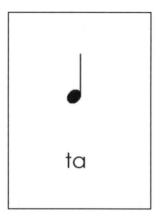

Additional Note Cards

Two eighth notes = 1 beat. Clap two times while saying "ti, ti."

Half note = 2 beats. Clap one time, then turn right hand over and say "two."

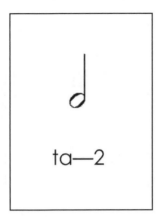

Dotted half note = 3 beats. Clap one time, then turn right hand over and say "two, three."

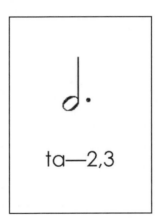

Whole note = 4 beats. Clap one time, turn the right hand over and say "two, three, four."

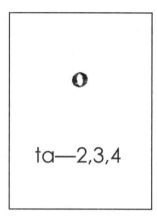

Quarter rest = one beat, no sound. Turn both hands over and whisper "rest."

CREATING YOUR OWN RHYTHM

Objectives: To increase the ability to decode symbols, visual tracking, eye–hand coordination, self expression, and interaction skills.

Materials needed: Individual laminated note cards.

Set up: The student and leader sit across and facing each other either on the floor or at a table.

Steps

1. Choose two note or rest cards.

2. Arrange them on the floor in front of the child.

3. Point to the first card and ask the child to clap and say the note rhythm, then the second.

4. Once the child masters this sequence, add more cards.

5. Ask the child to create a rhythm sequence that you then clap.

RHYTHM WORKSHEETS

Once the child has mastered the individual note cards, move on to the six rhythm worksheets featured later in this chapter. Below I describe the activities you can draw on to accompany the worksheets.

 CLAPPING THE RHYTHM

Objectives: To increase the ability to decode symbols, visual tracking, eye–hand coordination, self expression, and interaction skills.

Materials needed: Rhythm worksheets #1–6.

Set up: For pointing and prompting purposes, the student and leader should sit facing each other either on the floor or at a table. If it is too difficult for the leader to read the pattern upside down, the leader may elect to sit next to the child during this activity.

Steps

1. Introduce the first rhythm worksheet and encourage the child to clap the rhythm in order from left to right. Then move to the second line and again clap the rhythm from left to right.

2. Once the first sheet is mastered, work through all the sheets in order.

 ## PLAYING INSTRUMENTS TO THE RHYTHM WORKSHEETS

Once the rhythm worksheets have been mastered by clapping, you may encourage the child to play a rhythm instrument to the rhythm on each sheet. Some instruments work better than others for this activity. Rhythm sticks, gathering drums, paddle drums, and claves work quite well with this activity because it is easier to control the sound than an instrument such as an ocean drum.

Hints:

1. If it is too difficult initially for the child to play an instrument with the rhythm worksheets, you may first want to practice the notes and rests with the individual cards.

2. To make this activity easier:

   • Slow down the rhythm

- Model the rhythm on the same instrument that the child is using.

3. To make this activity more challenging:

   - Speed up the rhythm

   - Play a different instrument than the child.

 STOMPING THE BEATS

Once the patterns have been learned on the rhythm worksheets, you may want to encourage the child to try and do the beats with his feet. This activity can be quite challenging, but fun. Some of the children I have worked with were able to do this activity much better than me, and we always have fun trying!

- Quarter note = stomp one foot

- Eighth note = stomp one foot then the other

- Half note = stomp one foot, then touch toe to the floor on "two"

- Dotted half note = stomp one foot, then touch toe to the floor for "two, three"

- Whole note = stomp one foot, then touch toe to the floor for "two, three, four"

- Rest = whisper "rest", keep feet still.

Hints:

1. If it is difficult for the child to stomp his feet to the rhythm worksheets, you may first want to practice the notes and rests with the individual cards.

123

2. To make this activity easier, slow down the rhythm.

3. To make this activity more challenging:

- Speed up the rhythm

- Play the rhythm on the drum as the child stomps.

GUESS THAT RHYTHM

Objectives: To increase auditory awareness and interaction.

Materials needed: Individual note cards or rhythm worksheets.

Set up: I find this is best played with one adult and one child. The adult should sit with the child at a table or on the floor.

Steps

1. Depending on the ability of the child, place two or three individual note cards (see the beginning of this chapter) or two rhythm worksheets in front of the child.

2. Tell the child that you will be clapping the rhythm found on one of the cards in front of him.

3. Clap the rhythm, and then ask the child to point to the card containing the rhythm you just clapped.

4. Clap the rhythm again if needed.

5. Ask the child if he would like to clap a rhythm from one of the cards for you to identify.

Hint: To make this activity easier, use only two of the individual note cards to begin with. To make this activity more challenging, place more individual rhythm cards or more rhythm worksheets in front of the child at one time.

Rhythm Sheet #1

ta   ti ti   ta   ta

ti ti   ti ti   ta   ta

Rhythm Sheet #2

ta   ta   ti ti   ta

ti ti   ta   ti ti   ta—2

125

Rhythm Sheet #3

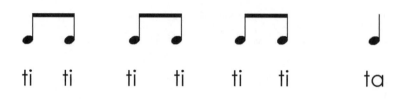

ti ti   ti ti   ti ti   ta

ta-2   ti ti   ta   ta-2,3,4

Rhythm Sheet #4

ta   rest   ti ti   rest

ta   ti ti   rest   rest   ta-2,3,4

Rhythm Sheet #5

rest   ti   ti   rest   ti   ti   ta   ta   ta

ti   ti   rest   ti   ti   rest   ta-2,3,4   ti   ti

Rhythm Sheet #6

Ti   ti   ti   ti   ti   ti   ti   ti   ta-2,3,4

ta-2   ta-2   ta   ti   ti   ta   rest

Chapter **7**

USING MUSIC TO IDENTIFY FEELINGS AND EMOTIONS

Identifying their own emotions and understanding the emotions of others can be a challenge for children with special needs, especially those on the autism spectrum. It is extremely difficult for a child to have appropriate interactions with others if he is unable to read their body language and sense what they are feeling.

The following activities may assist children in learning to understand their own feelings and learning to sense what others are feeling.

HOW DO YOU FEEL?

Use the traditional children's song *If You're Happy and You Know It* to sing about many different feelings and emotions.

Objectives: To identify feelings and emotions, increasing vocal skills.

Materials needed: None needed, but a recording of the song can be played, or singing can be accompanied on guitar, piano, autoharp, or Q-chord.

Set up: This can be done with an individual child or with a group of children.

Steps

1. Sing *If You're Happy and You Know It* as written making a happy face as the children sing.

2. Sing it again substituting "happy" for "sad." Ask the children to make a sad face as they sing.

3. Sing the song again using "angry." Encourage the children to make an angry face as they sing.

4. Continue using adjectives such as excited, nervous, sleepy, sick, etc.

5. Ask the children for suggestions!

PLAYING EMOTIONS ON INSTRUMENTS

Objectives: To identify feelings and emotions, increasing self expression.

Materials needed: A variety of rhythm instruments, and a recording of *If You're Happy and You Know It*, if needed.

Set up: This can be done with an individual child or with a group of children. Allow the children to choose a rhythm instrument that they would like to play.

Steps

1. Sing or play *If You're Happy and You Know It*. Encourage the child to play his instrument in a way that sounds "happy."

2. Play the song again substituting "sad" for "happy." Encourage the child to play his instrument in a way that sounds "sad."

3. Continue using adjectives for other feelings and emotions.

4. Ask the child for suggestions!

 MOVING TO EMOTIONS

Objectives: To identify feelings and emotions, increasing self expression.

Materials needed: A recording of *If You're Happy and You Know It*, if needed.

Set up: This can be done with an individual child or with a group of children. Allow plenty of room for each child to move.

Steps

1. Sing *If You're Happy and You Know It* using the following words:

    "If you're happy and you know it, dance around."

    Encourage the children to dance as if they feel "happy."

2. Sing the song again substituting "sad" for "happy." Encourage the children to dance as if they feel "sad."

3. Continue using adjectives for other feelings and emotions.

4. Ask the children for suggestions!

MOOD MUSIC

Objectives: To identify feelings and emotions, increasing self expression.

Materials needed: Recordings of different types of music that evoke feelings, such as songs in a minor key for "sad," faster songs in a major key for "happy," and so on. Try to vary the types of music (classical, classic rock, instrumental, etc.). Playing these songs or improvising would allow smoother transition between styles. This activity could be accomplished by moving to the music, playing on rhythm instruments or drawing what you hear on paper.

Set up: This can be done with an individual child or with a group of children.

Steps

1. Ask the child to listen to the song you are about to play. Encourage him to move, play or draw what he hears. Stop the music and ask the child to use a word to describe how the music made him feel.

2. Switch to another song or style of music. Encourage the child to move, play or draw what he hears. Stop the music and ask the child to use a word to describe how the music made him feel.

3. Continue through other emotions if wanted.

4. Ask the child which song he liked the most and why.

Chapter 8

MOVING TO MUSIC

It's usually not very hard to encourage a young child to move to music. Sounds and rhythms are irresistible to children, just turn on an upbeat song and watch the toes start to tap and bodies start to sway. Music is a great motivator and movement to music is quite natural and fun.

Children naturally learn by moving and playing. Movement benefits the whole child in many obvious areas such as motor coordination and fine and gross motor skill development, but it can also encourage growth in areas such as learning, cognition, language, interaction, self confidence, and self esteem.

Several types of music and movement experiences can be used depending on the needs of your child(ren). The songs and activities listed in this section fall into one of three categories: structured movement songs, movement and action songs and free movement songs and activities.

STRUCTURED MOVEMENT SONGS

Structured movement songs are songs with lyrics instructing the child how to move. A well-known, easy example of this type of activity is the *Hokey Pokey*. Structured movement songs are useful when working on listening skills, when learning directional concepts such as up, down, in, out, and body part identification. They can also be useful with children who may be a bit timid about getting involved in a free movement activity.

Two examples of structured movement songs are included in this book. I wrote and recorded both of them to encourage listening skills, motor coordination, learning directional concepts, and to encourage self expression through movement.

The first song, entitled *Up Down Boogie*, includes the directional concepts up, down, turn around, high and low. Sing and move to it slowly until the children become familiar with the motions, then try it faster. The lyrics, melody and chords can be found in the Sheet Music section at the end of the book.

The Freeze is the second example of a structured movement song. Movements in this song include wiggling, jumping, rubbing your tummy and of course—freezing! The lyrics, melody and chords for *The Freeze* can be found in the Sheet Music section at the end of the book. Recordings of these two songs and other structured movement to music songs can be found on my *Tunes for Moving* album, available on the *Music for Special Kids* website at www. musicforspecialkids.com.

Other examples of structured movement songs are:

- *Head, Shoulders, Knees and Toes*

- *Clap Along With Me* (see lyrics opposite)

- *Put Your Little Foot* (see lyrics opposite)

CLAP ALONG WITH ME

traditional song, unknown author

Find the tune on the internet, speak the lyrics in time, or sing it to the tune of *Row, Row, Row Your Boat.*

(Chorus) Clap, clap, clap your hands, Clap along with me
Clap, clap, clap your hands, Clap along with me.

1. Clap a little faster now, Clap along with me
   Clap a little faster now, Clap along with me.

   (Chorus) Clap, clap, clap your hands, Clap along with me
   Clap, clap, clap your hands, Clap along with me.

2. Clap a little slower now, Clap along with me
   Clap a little slower now, Clap along with me.

   (Chorus) Clap, clap, clap your hands, Clap along with me
   Clap, clap, clap your hands, Clap along with me.

PUT YOUR LITTLE FOOT

traditional song, unknown author

Find the tune on the internet or speak the lyrics in time. Add more verses such as "Put your hands up," or "Touch your shoulders," and so forth.

Put your little foot, put your little foot
Put your little foot right there.
Put your little foot, put your little foot,
Put your little foot right there.
Walk and walk and walk
And walk and turn.

Walk and walk and walk

And walk and turn.

MOVEMENT AND ACTION SONGS AND ACTIVITIES

Movement and action songs and activities are songs which encourage movement or hand motions, but do not necessarily give the specific movement instruction within the lyrics. They allow for some creativity in the type of movement while still retaining some structure. Movement and action songs and activities are good to use to stimulate gross and fine motor skills, to learn directional concepts, to stimulate cognitive skills, and to increase interaction and self expression.

Well-known examples of movement and action songs and activities you could use include *Eency Weency Spider*, *Shake My Sillies Out* (Raffi) and *The Chicken Dance*.

The songs and activities I describe in more detail are:

- *Hey, Mr. Knickerbocker*

- *The Grand Ol' Duke of York*

- *Animal Song*

- *Little Red Boat*

- *Happy Feet*

- *Metronome Moving*

- *Paddle Drum March*

- *Baby Steps, Giant Steps*

- *Standing for a Consonant*

HEY MR. KNICKERBOCKER

traditional rhythmic chant

1. Hey, Mr. Knickerbocker, boppity bop
   I feel so good with my boppity bop.
   I put that beat right into my feet!
   A one and a two and a three and a four.

2. Hey Mr. Knickerbocker, boppity bop
   I feel so good with my boppity bop.
   I put that beat right into my knees!
   A one and a two and a three and a four.

   (Repeat using hands, head, hips, shoulders, etc.)

THE GRAND OL' DUKE OF YORK

The Grand Ol' Duke of York is a traditional song that encourages marching and lots of other movement. Lyrics and actions can be found below and the lyrics, melody and chords can be found in the Sheet Music section at the end of the book.

   Oh, the Grand Ol' Duke of York, he had ten thousand men.
   He marched them up to the top of the hill, and he marched
      them down again.
   And when you're up, you're up.
   And when you're down, you're down.
   And when you're only halfway up,
   You're neither up nor down!

Movements

Pretend you're a soldier and march along with *The Grand Ol' Duke of York*. Be sure to stand tall and raise your arms when marching to the top of the hill, and crouch down low when you march back down the hill.

The *Animal Song* and *Little Red Boat* are two movement and action songs that I wrote and recorded to use when working on motor coordination, gross motor skills, interaction, and self expression. Lyrics and hand motions can be found below, and the lyrics, melody and chords for both songs can be found in the Sheet Music section at the end of the book.

 ANIMAL SONG

1. Why don't elephants fly? Can you tell me the reason why?
    They're too big, to even try.
    We know that elephants don't fly. What do they do?
    They stomp around in the zoo!

2. Birds don't swim under the sea. Can you tell me why that would be?
    They need their wings to fly free.
    We know that birds don't swim. Do you know why?
    They fly around, in the sky.
    We know that elephants don't fly. What do they do?
    They stomp around in the zoo!

3. Frogs don't waddle on their feet. It really wouldn't that look neat.
    They hop around, up and down.

Frogs don't waddle on their feet. What do they do?

They hop around like me and you.

We know that birds don't swim. Do you know why?

They fly around, in the sky.

We know that elephants don't fly. What do they do?

They stomp around in the zoo!

4. Why don't chickens slither like a snake? That might be a big mistake.

They strut around, and peck at the ground.

Chickens don't slither like a snake. What do they do?

They strut around saying "cock-a-doodle-doo."

Frogs don't waddle on their feet. What do they do?

They hop around like me and you.

We know that birds don't swim. Do you know why?

They fly around, in the sky.

We know that elephants don't fly. What do they do?

They stomp around in the zoo!

Motions and movements

Talk through the song demonstrating a motion or movement for each of the animals, such as fly = flap arms, stomp = stomp feet, swim = move arms as if swimming, and so forth.

After demonstrating the motions, speak the lyrics to the song again, encouraging the children to perform the motions and movements.

Once the motions have been mastered while speaking the lyrics, play the recorded song and have fun!

LITTLE RED BOAT

(*Chorus*) Splashing and rolling the waves of the sea,
Come right up and they tickle me.
Oh, sailing around in the deep blue sea,
I'm a little red boat in the big, blue sea.

1. A clam on the bottom has just opened up,
   But when he sees us he slams back shut.
   The seagulls are flying around in the sky,
   Wouldn't it be fun to be able to fly!

(*Chorus*)

2. The fish in the ocean are swimming around,
   Darting away from every sound.
   A friendly dolphin comes gliding up,
   He's just diving and playing and having fun!

(*Chorus*)

Motions and movements

During the chorus section, encourage the children to sway back and forth as if their boat was gently swaying in the waves.

- *Little red boat* = hold hands up close together as if measuring something small

- *Big blue sea* = open arms wide

- *A clam on the bottom has just opened up* = hold hands palm together, and then open them

- *When he sees us he slams back shut* = close hands quickly

- *The fish in the ocean are swimming around* = put palms of hands together and move them back and forth

- *A friendly dolphin comes gliding up* = keep hands palm together and make diving motions with them.

 HAPPY FEET

Objectives: To increase motor skills, motor coordination, listening skills, and self expression.

Materials needed: A gathering drum, paddle drum or other loud drum, mallets.

Set up: This activity works well with one child or with a group of children. It should be done in an area with ample room for each child to move.

Steps

1. Play the drum softly and ask the children how they might move their feet softly (tiptoe). Play the drum loudly and ask the children how they might move their feet loudly (stomp). Practice playing fast and slow and stop and go.

2. Begin playing the drum, changing between soft, loud, fast slow, stop and go. Give plenty of time on each adjective for the children to adjust their movement appropriately.

3. Play a rhythm such as fast, fast, slow—fast, fast, slow. See if the children begin to copy the beat with their feet.

4. Ask if someone else would like to be the drum leader!

METRONOME MOVING

Objectives: To increase motor skills, motor coordination, listening skills, and self expression.

Materials needed: A metronome.

Set up: This activity works well with one child or with a group of children. It should be done in an area with ample room for each child to move.

Steps

1. Introduce the child to the metronome.

2. Let him hear a slow beat (tempo) and then a faster beat (tempo).

3. Encourage the child to begin moving when you turn the metronome on and to move to the beat. If the beat is fast, move fast. If the beat slows down, slow down too.

4. Let the metronome stay on each setting long enough that the child can explore different types of movement to each tempo.

 PADDLE DRUM MARCH

Objectives: To increase motor skills, motor coordination, listening skills, interaction, and self expression.

Materials needed: A recorded marching song. *Yankee Doodle* or *This Old Man* are two well-known children's songs that may work well for this activity. A paddle drum and mallet for each child and leader.

Set up: This activity works well with one child or with a group of children. It should be done in an area with ample room for each child to move.

Steps

1. Ask the children to stand in a circle and to practice marching in place.

2. Turn on the music and practice marching in place.

3. Hand each child a paddle drum.

4. Encourage the children to start marching, then try to beat the drum as they march. Counting in a slow steady march beat may help.

5. Turn on the recorded march and encourage children to march in place and beat the paddle drum.

6. Once the children have mastered marching in place, march in a circle around the room!

Hint: If a child has difficulty marching while playing the drum:

1. Hold the paddle drum for the child as he marches and beats the drum.

2. Give physical assistance with the child's arm beating the drum.

3. Tell the child just to move around the room while beating the drum.

Remember to make this a successful activity for each child by modifying the movements to fit the abilities of each individual.

BABY STEPS, GIANT STEPS

Objectives: To increase motor skills, motor coordination, listening skills, and to increase awareness of the musical terms *forte* and *piano*.

Materials needed: A gathering drum.

Set up: This activity works well with one child or with a group of children. It should be done in an area with ample room for each child to move.

Steps

1. Ask the children to sit around the gathering drum.

2. Play the drum softly. Ask the children to describe how you are playing.

3. Tell the children that another word for playing softly is *piano*.

4. Play the drum louder. Ask the children to describe how you are playing.

5. Tell the children that another word for playing loudly is *forte*.

6. Ask the children to stand up.

7. Explain that you will be playing the drum *piano* and *forte*.

8. When they hear *piano* ask the children to take baby steps in a circle around the drum.

9. When they hear *forte* ask the children to take giant steps in a circle around the drum.

10. Begin playing, giving verbal prompts of *piano* and *forte* as you change dynamics. Give ample time on each dynamic for the child to take the appropriate steps.

11. Once the children have mastered the concept, remove the verbal prompts and allow them to follow the cues from the music.

STANDING FOR A CONSONANT

Objectives: To increase motor skills, motor coordination, listening skills, and identifying specific consonants or consonant blends.

Materials needed: A recording of a song, with repetitive consonants or consonant blends such as *My Bonnie Lies Over the Ocean* or *Freddy the Frog* (see the Sheet Music section at the end of the book for the latter). Singing and playing these songs will also allow you to slow down or speed up based on the needs of your group.

Set up: This activity works well with one child or with a group of children. It should be done in an area with ample room for each child to move.

Steps

1. Print the lyrics of this song in large print on a large piece of paper.

2. Highlight the consonant or consonant blend that you would like the children to watch for.

3. Sing through the song and point to the words. Accent the consonant or consonant blend as you sing it.

4. Explain to the children that you will now sing the song and point to the words, and every time you point to a highlighted consonant or consonant blend, they are to stand up and quickly sit back down.

5. Once the children have mastered it while you are singing and pointing, simply sing it and see if they can identify the consonant blend just by hearing it.

Hint: If this activity is physically too difficult for your child or children, you may encourage them to shake a rhythm instrument, clap hands, or stomp feet when the consonant or consonant blend is sung.

FREE MOVEMENT SONGS AND ACTIVITIES

Free movement songs and activities include creative movement or dance to different styles of music and musical activities structured to allow self expression through movement. There usually needs to be some structure so that the activity doesn't get out of control, but still allows spontaneous movement. Of the three types of activities outlined in this Moving to Music chapter, the free movement songs and activities provide the greatest opportunity for self expression, but can also be useful for stimulating language skills, motor skills, and coordination.

 ## PHYSICALLY EXPLORING THE MUSIC

Music has the inherent ability to affect mood and evoke feelings. At the same time, some music is stimulating and some is calming.

Tapping in to all of these factors by providing a wide range of music and styles can allow children to express themselves in ways that they may not have found possible before.

Objectives: To increase self expression and to stimulate motor skills and motor coordination.

Materials needed: Recordings of several different styles and types of music. This certainly does not need to be children's music! Possibilities include pieces from Tchaikovsky's *Nutcracker Suite*, *Maple Leaf Rag* by Scott Joplin, *Daybreak Vision* by R. Carlos Nakai, *Caribbean Party Music* from Autumn Hill Records, and *Planet Drum* by Mickey Hart from The World/Rykodisk/Mickey Hart Series.

Set up: This activity works well with one child or with a group of children. It should be done in an area with ample room for each child to move. I like to do this in a room with a large wall mirror, as it seems my children are more excited to move when they can watch themselves in the mirror.

Steps

1. Play several minutes of music from one of the recordings. Encourage the children to listen to the music and move any way the music makes them feel.

2. To encourage language skills, at the completion of the movement activity, ask each child to describe how the dancing felt. Play a little bit of each recording and ask each child to describe the sound of the music.

SCARF DANCE

Using the same music and steps above, encourage the children to use one or two scarves and to move and wave them while dancing.

DRUM DANCING

Objectives: To increase motor skills, motor coordination, listening skills, and self expression.

Materials needed: Several different types of drums if available and mallets.

Set up: This activity works well with one child or with a group of children. It should be done in an area with ample room for each child to move.

Steps

1. Tell the children that you are going to be telling a musical story with your drum. You won't be talking, but you'll be telling a story with the rhythm as you play.

2. Encourage the children to listen to the drum play and to copy the drum with their movement. Use dynamics, tempo and rhythm to create a musical story for them to move to.

3. Upon completion, ask the children for their ideas on what the story was about!

EXPLORING HOW OUR BODIES MOVE WITH MUSIC

Objectives: To increase body awareness, motor skills, and motor coordination.

Materials needed: A recording of soft, non-obtrusive instrumental music, such as *Tunes for Relaxation* by Pamela Ott, *Gymnopedie #1* by Erik Satie, or *The Most Relaxing Classical Music in the Universe* by Denon Records.

Set up: This activity works well with one child or with a group of children and should be done in an area with ample room for each child to move.

Steps

1. While playing soft instrumental music in the background, tell the children that they are going to see how many different ways their bodies can move.

2. Start by standing, taking one arm and moving it in whatever way possible; lift it up, down, rotate the palm up, then palm down, swing it gently from side to side. Repeat with the other arm.

3. Move to the head. Tilt it left, then right, gently roll it in a circle, look down with your chin on your chest, then up.

4. Try the legs now. Take one leg, lift it up, and then set it down. Swing it to the left, then the right. Swing it in front, then behind. Lift the knee to your chest. Repeat with the other leg.

5. Now sit down in a chair and try the above exercises again. Can your arms, head and legs move the same way while sitting?

6. Now move down to the floor on your hands and knees. How can your arms, head and legs move from this position?

7. If room allows, lay on the floor on your back. How can your arms, head and legs move from this position?

8. At the end of the exercise, if working on language skills, ask the children the difference in the movement of their arms, head and legs in each position.

 ## MUSICAL COLORS AND SHAPES

Depending on the concept or objective you're working on with your child, print a variety of colors or shapes. Laminate them for durability and fix them to the floor in a circle with masking tape. Note: Laminated sheets may be too slippery on some surfaces.

Objectives: To increase listening skills, attending skills, motor skills, motor coordination, shape, and color identification.

Materials needed: Recordings of different types of music, 8.5 x 10 inch (20 x 25 cm) color and shape cards.

Set up: This activity works well with one child or with a group of children. It should be done in an area with ample room for each child to move.

Steps

1. In the manner of musical chairs, arrange more cards than children playing in a large circle.

2. Instruct the children to move around the circle (not stepping on the cards) while the music is playing and to stop next to a card when the music stops.

3. Ask each child if he can identify the shape or color on the card he is standing next to.

4. If the child has trouble identifying the color or shape, ask him if he would like to ask someone else for a clue or for the answer.

Chapter **9**

LEARNING MUSICAL CONCEPTS

With the exception of some of the rhythm activities the majority of the activities in this book have used songs, musical activities and instruments to encourage growth in non-musical goals such as communication, motor skills, attending skills, and interaction. You may find that your child is ready and able to begin to learn musical concepts, which may prepare him for music lessons at some point.

The following musical activities can introduce children to musical terms such as tempo, rhythm and dynamics, and note value and recognition.

DYNAMICS AND TEMPO ON THE DRUM

Objectives: To increase knowledge of musical dynamics and tempo, listening skills, and attending skills.

Materials needed: Several different types of drums if available, and mallets.

Set up: This activity works well with one child or with a group of children. It should be done in an area with ample room for each child to move.

Steps: Dynamics

1. Talk to the children about the musical terms *forte* (loud) and *piano* (soft).

2. Explain that during this activity you will be playing either *forte* or *piano*. Ask the children to clap their hands *forte* and then to clap their hands *piano*.

3. Practice playing *forte* and *piano*. Ask the children to identify the dynamic while you play by using the word *forte* or *piano*. Be sure to play at the same tempo for both *forte* and *piano* so that the children will not confuse them with the tempo terms below.

4. Add a movement component by playing *forte*, saying *forte* out loud and asking the children to stand and stomp their feet to the beat.

5. Then play *piano*, say *piano* out loud and ask the children to stand and tiptoe to the beat.

Steps: Tempo

1. Talk to the children about the musical terms *presto* (fast) and *largo* (slow).

2. Explain that during this activity you will be playing either *presto* or *largo*. Ask the children to clap their hands *presto* and then to clap their hands *largo*.

LEARNING MUSICAL CONCEPTS

3. Practice playing *presto* and *largo*. Ask the children to identify the dynamic while you play by using the word *presto* or *largo*. Be sure to play at the same dynamic for both *presto* and *largo* so that the children will not confuse them with the dynamic terms above.

4. Add a movement component by saying and playing *presto* and asking the children to stand and move rapidly around the drum to the beat.

5. Then say and play *largo* and ask the children to stand and move slowly around the drum to the beat.

MUSICAL NOTES

Depending on the concept or objective you're working on with your child, print a variety of notes (quarter, half, whole) or musical notations (treble clef, bass clef, staff, rests, time signature, etc.). Laminate them for durability and fix them to the floor in a circle with masking tape. Note: Laminated sheets may be too slippery on some surfaces.

Objectives: To increase listening skills, attending skills, motor skills, motor coordination, musical note or notation identification.

Materials needed: Recordings of different types of music, 8.5 x 10 inch (20 x 25 cm) musical note or notation cards.

Set up: This activity works well with one child or with a group of children. It should be done in an area with ample room for each child to move.

Steps

1. In the manner of musical chairs, arrange more cards than children playing in a large circle.

2. Instruct the children to move around the circle (not stepping on the cards) while the music is playing and to stop next to a card when the music stops.

3. Ask each child if he can identify the musical note or notation on the card he is standing next to.

4. If the child has trouble identifying the musical note or notation, ask him if he would like to ask someone else for a clue or for the answer.

 NOTES ON A STAFF

A musical staff contains five lines and four spaces. Create a musical staff about 5 feet (150 cm) wide on the floor using masking tape.

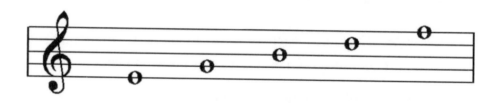

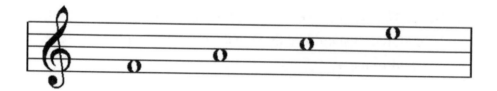

Objectives: To increase listening skills, attending skills, motor skills, motor coordination, and note placement on a staff.

Materials needed: A xylophone, glockenspiel, handbells, or another instrument that can play individual melody notes, masking tape.

Set up: This activity works well with one child or with a small group of children.

Steps

1. In addition to the 5 foot musical staff taped to the floor create a musical staff on an 8.5 x 10 inch (20 x 25 cm) piece of paper and laminate it.

2. Talk to the children about the musical staff and ask them to count the lines.

3. Show them the four spaces between the lines and ask them to count the spaces.

4. Ask each child to come up and point first to a line, and then to a space.

5. Talk to the children about how each line and space represents a note in the musical alphabet A, B, C, D, E, F or G.

6. Ask one child to point to the bottom line and play an E on the melody instrument.

7. Ask one child to point to the first space (above the bottom line) and play an F on the melody instrument.

8. Continue in this way for the remaining lines and spaces.

9. Talk to the children about the staff on the floor made of masking tape.

10. Explain to the children that they are going to be a note on the staff.

11. Ask one of the children to go and stand on the bottom or first line. As the child steps on the first line, say E and play an E on the melody instrument.

12. Ask another child to stand on the first space. As the child steps on the first space, say F and play an F on the melody instrument.

13. Continue in this way for the remaining lines and spaces.

Hints: There are many opportunities to modify this activity based on the abilities and interest levels of your student(s).

1. To simplify this activity, teach only one or two notes per session or model the appropriate position for each note.

2. To make this activity more challenging, teach the acronym for the treble clef line notes: Elvis's Guitar Broke Down Friday, and the acronym for the treble clef space notes: FACE. Present more notes per session or more combinations of lines and spaces per session.

 ## STACCATO AND LEGATO

To teach the concept of *staccato* (short and detached) and *legato* (smooth and connected), try the following activity.

Objectives: To increase listening skills, attending skills, motor skills, motor coordination, and identification of the terms *staccato* and *legato*.

Materials needed: Guiro or rhythm sticks for *staccato*, autoharp, keyboard, Q-chord or guitar for *legato*.

Set up: This activity works well with one child or with a group of children. It should be done in an area with ample room for each child to move.

Steps

1. Explain the musical terms *staccato* and *legato* to the children. Staccato means to play in a short, detached manner and *legato* means to play in a smooth connected manner.

2. Model a *staccato* sound on the guiro or rhythm sticks. Ask the children how they would move to this type of sound (hop, jump, move then freeze, etc.).

3. Model a *legato* sound on the autoharp, keyboard, Q-chord or guitar. Ask the children how they would move to this type of sound (glide, twirl, sweep, etc.).

4. Ask the children to stand in a circle and to listen to the music you are about to play.

5. Instruct them to hop, jump, move then freeze, and so forth when they hear a *staccato* sound and to glide, twirl, sweep, and so on when they hear a *legato* sound.

Hint: Another way to present this concept is to allow the children to pick a rhythm instrument and to play along with you, matching *staccato* and *legato* on their instruments.

Chapter **10**

QUIET TIME ACTIVITIES

MUSIC FOR RELAXATION

Just as music can be used to cause stimulation (just think of how you feel when you hear some of your favorite upbeat music!), music can also be used to help individuals calm down and relax.

Children with special needs can be taught relaxation techniques that may assist them when their surroundings become too over-stimulating. Several of these exercises are outlined in the Relaxation Exercises section below.

Slow and relaxing music can also be used as background music while participating in other activities. This calming background music can assist in keeping the noise level down and can be used as a measure of vocal levels—"let's keep our voices at the same level as the music." The Quiet Time Activities section below lists activities that can be done using quiet time music in the background.

How do you choose appropriate quiet time music? Music affects everyone differently, but there are a few things I would suggest.

- Use instrumental music. When you add words and complicated melodies to the music, it adds more elements for the brain to focus on, making it less calming.

- The arrangements should be fairly simple. The more instruments the more complicated the sound and again, more elements for the brain to focus on.

- Simple guitar, piano, flute, harp and cello sounds can provide just the right amount of interest but not be over-stimulating.

- Use music recorded at or about the resting heart rate (60–70 beats per minute).

The following are a few suggestions of quiet time music. You may create your own compilation from a variety of recordings as you may find some tracks on individual recordings less relaxing than others.

- Guitar for Relaxation—Enrique Granados RCA Music 2000

- Cello for Relaxation—RCA Records 2001

- The Ultimate Most Relaxing Classics for Kids in the Universe—Denon Records 2007

- Across an Ocean of Dreams—Real Music 2002

- Tunes for Relaxation—Pamela Ott 2008

RELAXATION EXERCISES

Many children with special needs experience a high level of stress in their daily life, from the over-stimulation of sights, sounds, and touch to possible struggles with interaction and self esteem. Equipping them with strategies to "self-calm" can be enlightening and empowering.

WHOLE BODY QUIET TIME

Objectives: To learn how to quiet down the whole body, to learn relaxation strategies, and to relax.

Materials needed: A quiet time recording.

Set up: This activity works well with one child or with a group of children. It should be done in an area where each child can spread out and not bump anyone else.

Steps

1. Encourage the children to sit in a circle on the floor.

2. Turn on the quiet time recording. Ask the children to remain quiet, to listen to the music and to listen to your instructions.

3. Ask the children to:

    o   close their eyes and take a deep breath, and then slowly let it out

    o   slowly roll their heads around in a circle

    o   gently stretch one shoulder up and down, and then the other shoulder

    o   roll the arms around in a big, slow circle, and then rest their hands in their lap

    o   breathe deep again and then gently lay down on the floor

    o   slowly lift one leg up and down and then the other

    o   roll one foot at a time around from the ankle

    o   lay still and continue to take nice deep breaths.

GET TIGHT, GET LOOSE

Objectives: To increase muscle awareness, to learn relaxation strategies, and to relax.

Materials needed: A quiet time recording.

Set up: This activity works well with one child or with a group of children. It should be done in an area where each child can spread out and not bump anyone else.

Steps

1. Encourage the children to lie down on the floor or on a mat and turn on the quiet time recording.

2. Ask the children to think about their toes. Ask them if they can bend their toes down towards the floor and make them feel tight.

3. Ask the children to hold them tight until you count to three, and then let them loose—relax.

4. Ask the children to think about their upper legs. Ask them if they can make their upper legs (thighs) tight.

5. Again, ask the children to hold them tight until you count to three, and then let them loose—relax.

6. Continue this process with the tummy, arms (squeeze against the body), hands and face.

7. After completion, allow them to lay quietly until you count to ten.

TUMMY BREATHING

Taking slow, deep breaths can facilitate the relaxation process. To assist children in learning how to take deep breaths, try this activity.

Objectives: To encourage deep breathing, to learn relaxation strategies and to relax.

Materials needed: A quiet time recording.

Set up: This activity works well with one child or with a group of children. It should be done in an area where each child can spread out and not bump anyone else.

Steps

1. Ask the children to lie on their back on the floor or on a mat and turn on the quiet time recording.

2. Tell the children to pretend that their tummies are balloons.

3. Ask them to practice taking a deep breath though their mouths and see if they can get their tummies to grow like a balloon.

4. If that is difficult for them, ask them to place their hand on their tummy and see if they can move it up and down by breathing.

5. Once they are able to do this, ask them to wait to take a really deep breath until you say breathe.

6. Say breathe calmly—in time to the music, then say hold, and then say let it out.

7. Wait for ample time between deep breaths for the children to get ready for the next breath.

QUIET TIME ACTIVITIES

Play calming music in the background to set the tone for these activities.

 TOUCH AND ADD

Objectives: To increase sequencing skills, to increase attending skills, and to relax.

Materials needed: A quiet time recording.

Set up: This activity works well with one child or with a group of children.

Steps

1. Encourage the children to sit in a circle.

2. Explain that while the quiet time music is on, no one should talk, just watch with their eyes.

3. Quietly stand up, touch an object in the room, such as a chair, and then sit back down.

4. The next person in the circle will stand up, touch the chair and then touch one more item in the room.

5. Go around the circle and ask each child to touch the objects previously touched and to add one of their own.

6. Continue until the order is forgotten, and then start over!

Hint: To make this game easier, the leader may elect to touch one object, and then allow the next child in the circle to touch that same object—repeating the motion for all children in the circle.

WALK THAT LINE

Using masking tape, make a continuous line on the floor that bends, has straight sections and zig zags.

Objectives: To increase motor coordination, to learn relaxation strategies, and to relax.

Materials needed: A quiet time recording, masking tape.

Set up: This activity works well with one child or with a group of children.

Steps

1. Tell the children that while the quiet time music is playing, you will all try not to talk.

2. Show the children the masking tape line on the floor.

3. Explain that when the music starts, everyone will walk slowly and single file on the line, tying not to fall off.

4. Upon reaching the end, encourage the children to turn around and go back the opposite way.

5. Once that pattern is mastered, turn the music off, and ask the children for their suggestions in creating a new, more challenging line!

RHYME TIME

Objectives: To increase expressive language skills, to increase interaction, to increase attending skills, and learning to use a quiet voice.

Materials needed: A quiet time recording.

Set up: This activity works well with one child or with a group of children.

Steps

1. Talk about rhyming words and how they sound alike.

2. Give examples of rhyming words and ask the children for suggestions.

3. Tell the children that you are going to turn on quiet music and when the quiet music is on you all will whisper.

4. Turn the music on and whisper a one-syllable word, such as hat.

5. Ask the children to raise their hand if they know a word that rhymes with hat.

6. Point to a child with his hand up and ask him to whisper his rhyming word.

7. Ask if anyone else would like to be the leader and whisper a word.

 MATCH THIS

Objectives: To increase visual awareness, to increase attending skills, and learning to use a quiet voice.

Materials needed: A quiet time recording, pictures of faces from magazines that have been pasted onto construction paper (tough, coarse, colored paper) and then cut in half.

Set up: This activity works well with one child or with a group of children who work well together.

Steps

1. Mix the face halves and place them face up on a table or on the floor.

2. Encourage the children to pick one half face and then try to find the matching half.

3. For variety, try using pictures of cars, houses, animals, or musical instruments!

 MUSICAL CRAYONS

Objectives: To increase self expression, to increase language skills, and to increase fine motor skills.

Materials needed: A quiet time recording, a large piece of paper, crayons for each child.

Set up: This activity works well with one child or with a group of children. The children should be allowed plenty of space to draw and to be creative.

Steps

1. Provide the children with several pieces of blank paper and a variety of crayons.

2. Pick several styles of music including some with fast tempos, some with slow tempos, some with a happy sound (such as ragtime or boogie) and some with a sad sound (pieces in a minor key).

169

3. Ask the children to take one piece of paper and draw something that reflects how the music makes them feel. Play 2–3 minutes of each type of music.

4. Once the drawings are completed, go back and play a short excerpt of each type of music and talk about how it made them feel, what they drew and why.

Hint: Finger paint can be used instead of crayons if you are brave!

FINISH MY FACE

Using the half pictures of faces found in the *Match This* game, place one half picture of a face on a sheet of white paper. Encourage the children to finish the face on the other part of the paper. Help them to finish the outline of the face first, and then add the nose, eyes, mouth and hair.

TOUCH BAGS

Objectives: To increase tactile awareness, to increase attending skills, and to increase reasoning skills.

Materials needed: A quiet time recording, lunch-sized paper bags— each filled with a distinctive feeling item such as cotton balls, tennis ball, spoon, rubber band, pen, napkin, etc.

Set up: This activity works well with one child or with a group of children.

Steps

1. As you are sitting in a circle, remind the children not to talk while the music is playing.

2. Take one of the bags and pass it around the circle, allowing time for each child to reach in and touch the object(s) in the bag.

3. When the bag gets back to the leader, turn off the music and ask the children to guess what was in the bag!

4. Repeat with the remaining bags.

 SHADOW DANCING

Objectives: To increase motor coordination and allow opportunities for self expression.

Materials needed: A quiet time recording, a light or lamp.

Set up: This activity works well with one child or with a group of children, but is best performed one at a time with the others watching.

Steps

1. Identify a big blank wall.

2. Posture a light in proximity to the wall with ample space between the light and the wall for a child to move and dance.

3. Talk to the children about shadows and how they are made.

4. Model your shadow and show the children what your shadow looks like when you move and dance.

5. Tell them you are going to turn on quiet time music and ask them to watch and use their quiet voices.

6. Ask for a volunteer to do a shadow dance!

THE CALM SONG

The Calm Song is a song I wrote and recorded as a structured movement song (see the first part of Chapter 8 on Moving to Music) to encourage deep breathing and relaxation. The lyrics and motions are listed below and the melody and chords can be found in the Sheet Music section at the end of the book. The lyrics can also be chanted rhythmically if preferred.

Now close your eyes, relax and breathe deep.
Gently roll your head around, move your shoulders up and
    down.
Then lift your hands, up very high,
Slowly bring them down, touch your hands to the ground.
Sometimes we move like the wind, blowing around.
And sometimes we're like the sun, shining high in the sky.
But sometimes we need to slow down,
Floating like clouds in the sky.
Then like raindrops from a gentle spring rain,
Softly we all fall down.

Movements

Follow movements in the lyrics adding a gentle sway of the arms and body for "Sometimes we move like the wind." Lift arms in an arc over your head for "Sometimes we're like the sun." Move fingers down as if raindrops and gently fall to the ground for "Softly we all fall down."

SHEET MUSIC

Hello Song

(to the tune of Goodnight Ladies)

Hel - lo And - rew!   Hel - lo And - rew!   Hel - lo And - rew!

How   are   you   to - day?

Turkey in the Straw (the doo doo song)

traditional

Doo doo   doo   doo   doo   doo doo   doo   doo   doo doo doo

doo doo doo doo doo doo   doo   doo   doo   doo doo   doo   doo   doo   doo   doo

doo   doo   doo   doo   doo   doo   doo   doo   doo   doo   doo   doo   doo   doo.

Doo   doo   doo   doo   doo   doo   doo   doo   doo   doo   doo   doo

doo   doo   doo   doo   doo   doo   doo   doo   doo   doo   doo doo doo

doo   doo   doo   doo   doo   doo   doo   doo   doo   doo.

Ode to Joy

Ludwig van Beethoven

Ooh la ooh la ooh la ooh la ooh la ooh la ooh la la

Ooh la ooh la ooh la ooh la ooh la ooh la ooh la la

Dum Dum Da Da

traditional

Dum dum da da, da dum dum da da, da dum dum da, da, dee

dum. Dum dum da da, da dum dum da, da, da

dum dum da da dee dum.

Hey Bob A Needle

traditional

Hey bob a nee—dle, bob a nee—dle bob a nee—dle bob a,

Hey bob a nee—dle, bob a nee—dle bob a nee—dle bob a,

Hey bob a nee—dle, bob a nee—dle bob a nee—dle bob a,

Hey bob a nee—dle, bob a nee—dle bob a nee—dle bob a,

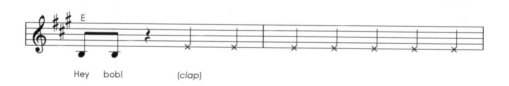

Hey bob!   (clap)

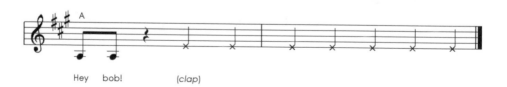

Hey bob!   (clap)

Waddley Ah Cha

traditional

Wad—dle—y ah — cha, wad—dle—y ah — cha, doo—dle—y do,

doo—dle—y do. Wad—dle—y ah — cha, wad—dle—y ah —cha

doo— dle — y do, doo— dle — y do, Sim — pl — est song there

Is —n't much to it, All you got —ta do is doo—dle — y do it.

I like the rest, but the part I like best is

Doo—dle — y doo — dle — y doo. Whoo!

The Bear

traditional

The o—ther day, (the o—ther day) I met a

bear, (I met a bear) a great big bear, (a great big bear) a—way up

there, (a—way up there) The o—ther day I met a

bear, a great big bear a—way out there.

2.   He looked at me (he looked at me), I looked at him (I looked at him).
He sized up me (he sized up me), I sized up him (I sized up him).
He looked at me, I looked at him. He sized up me I sized up him.

3.   He said to me (he said to me), "Why don't you run?" (why don't you run?).
"I see you ain't" (I see you ain't), "got any gun" (got any gun).
He said to me "Why don't you run? I see you ain't got any gun."

4.   And so I ran (and so I ran), away from there (away from there).
But right behind (but right behind) me was that bear (me was that bear).
And so I ran away from there, but right behind me was that bear.

5.   Ahead of me (ahead of me), I saw a tree (I saw a tree).
A great big tree (a great big tree), Oh glory be (oh glory be).
Ahead of me I saw a tree. A great big tree oh, glory be.

6.   The nearest branch (the nearest branch), was ten feet up (was ten feet up).
I'd have to jump (I'd have to jump), and trust my luck (and trust my luck).
The nearest branch was ten feet up, I'd have to jump and trust my luck.

7.   And so I jumped (and so I jumped), into the air (into the air)
But I missed that branch (but I missed that branch), away up there (away up there).
And so I jumped into the air, but I missed that branch away up there.

8.   Now don't you fret (now don't you fret), now don't you frown (now don't you frown)
'Cuz I caught that branch ('cuz I caught that branch), on the way back down (on the way back down).
Now don't you fret, now don't you frown. 'Cuz I caught that branch on the way back down.

9.   That's all there is (that's all there is), there ain't no more (there ain't no more)
So what the heck (so what the heck), are you singing for (are you singing for)?
That's all there is, there ain't no more, so what the heck are you singing for?

Ravioli

traditional

Refrain: Rav — i — o — li, I like ra — vi — o —li. Rav — i — o — li,

It's the best for me. **Do I have it on my chin?**

Yes, you have it on your chin. **On my chin?** On your chin. Oh — oh!

2.   Refrain (together)
    Do I have it in my hair? Yes, you have it in your hair! **In my hair?** In your hair.
    On my chin? On your chin. Ohhhh!

3.   Refrain (together)
    Do I have it in my ears? Yes, you have it in your ears! **In my ears?** In your ears.
    In my hair? In your hair.
    On my chin? On your chin. Ohhhh!

4.   Refrain (together)
    Do I have it on my shirt? Yes, you have it on your shirt! **On my shirt?** On your shirt.
    In my ears? In your ears.
    In my hair? In your hair.
    On my chin? On your chin. Ohhhh!

5.   Refrain (together)
    Do I have it on my pants? Yes, you have it on your pants. **On my pants?** On your pants.
    Do I have it on my shirt? Yes, you have it on your shirt.
    In my ears? In your ears.
    In my hair? In your hair.
    On my chin? On your chin. Ohhhh!

6.   Refrain (together)
    Do I have it on my toes? Yes, you have it on your toes. **On my toes?** On your toes.
    Do I have it on my pants? Yes, you have it on your pants.
    Do I have it on my shirt? Yes, you have it on your shirt.
    In my ears? In your ears.
    In my hair? In your hair.
    On my chin? On your chin. Ohhhh!

7.   Refrain (together)
    Do I have it on the wall? Yes, you have it on the wall. **On the wall?** On the wall.
    Do I have it on my toes? Yes, you have it on your toes
    Do I have it on my pants? Yes, you have it on your pants.
    Do I have it on my shirt? Yes, you have it on your shirt.
    In my ears? In your ears.
    In my hair? In your hair.
    On my chin? On your chin. Ohhhh!

Add additional verses if you wish and end by singing the refrain one more time!

Months of the Year #1

traditional

Jan — u — a — ry, Feb — ru — a — ry, March and Ap — ril,

May, June, and Ju — ly. Aug — gust, Sep — tem — ber, Oct — to — ber

too. No — vem—ber and De — cem — ber, are the twelve months of the

year. Nine months of which are our Kind — der — gar — ten year.

Months of the Year #3 (to Michael Finnegan)

Jan — u — a — ry, Feb — ru — a — ry, March and A — pril,

May, June Ju — ly, Au — gust, and Sept — tem — ber,

Oc — to — ber, No — vem — ber, and De — cem — ber,

These are the months of the year.

I Spy

Tune by Pamela Ott

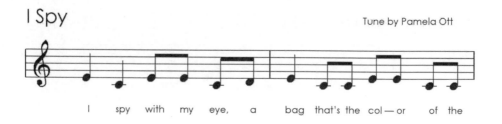

I spy with my eye, a bag that's the col — or of the

Grass. Throw it in the drum!

Give Yourself a Hug

words and music by Pamela Ott

Be good to your—self in ev — ery way. Tell your-self, you're O. K! Be

hap—py 'bout your-self and shout HOO-RAY! and give your—self a hug to — day!

Hug that knee, squeeze it tight. Hug those ar — ms too. Hug one foot and tell it

its all - right. Now you know just what to do!

Up Down Boogie

words and music by Pamela Ott

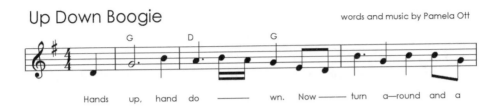

Hands up, hand do ——— wn. Now ——— turn a—round and a

round. And do the up down boo-gie woo-gie to the up down boo-gie woo-gie

sound. Hand up! Hands do ——— wn, we're gon—na

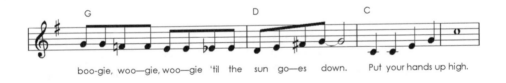

boo-gie, woo—gie, woo—gie 'til the sun go—es down. Put your hands up high.

try to touch the sky! Bring your hands back down. Try to touch the ground.

The Freeze

words and music by Pamela Ott

You want to wig—gle when the mus—ic plays, I like to wig—gle from my

head down to my toes. But list—en ve—ry close, pay att—en—tion if you please when the

mu — sic stops you freeze! Now it's time to wig—gle!

Stop! Now it's time to dance all a — round. Now it's time to

gig — gle. That's how you play the game!

The Grand Ol' Duke of York

traditional

Oh, the grand ol' Duke of York. He had ten thous—and men. he

marched them up to the top of the hill, and marched them down a—gain. And—

when you're up, you're up. And when you're down you're down, and when you're only halfway up,

You're nei — ther up or down!

Animal Song

words and music by Pamela Ott

Why don't el– eph—ants fly? Can you tell me the rea — son why?

They're too big, to e — ven fly. We know that

el — eph—ants don't fly what do they do? they

stomp a — round in the zoo.

Note: Additional verses are available in Chapter 8 Moving to Music

Little Red Boat

words and music by Pamela Ott

Spla-shin' and roll—in' the waves of the— sea. Come right up and they

Tick—le me. Oh—— sail — ing a — long in the deep blue sea, I'm a

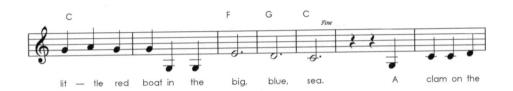

lit — tle red boat in the big, blue, sea. A clam on the

bot—tom has just op—ened up. But wh — en he sees us he

slams back shut! The sea—gulls are fly — ing a - round in the

sky. Oh, would—n't it be fun to be a — ble to fly?

189

Freddy the Frog

words and music by Pamela Ott

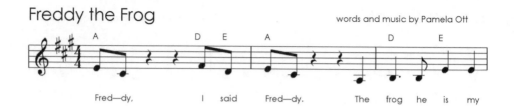

Fred—dy, I said Fred—dy. The frog he is my

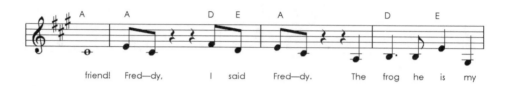

friend! Fred—dy, I said Fred—dy. The frog he is my

friend. He doesn't have wings like a bird. He doesn't have fins like a

fish. But he has four feet, that look pret — ty neat, and

Fred-dy he is my friend.

The Calm Song

words and music by Pamela Ott

1. Now close your eyes.
2. hands,

Re — lax and breathe deep.
up ver — y high.

Gent-ly roll your head a—round, move your should—ers up and
Slow—ly bring them down, touch your hands to the

down. Then lift your ground. Some-times we move like the wind,

blow—ing a — round. And some-times we're like the sun,

Shin—ing high in the sky. But some-times we need to slow down,

Float—ting like clouds in the sky. Then like rain-drops from a

gen — tle spring rain, soft — ly we all fall down.